Anonymous

Standing Rules and Orders Adopted by the Legislative Assembly, and Approved by the Governor

Together with the joint standing orders of the two houses

Anonymous

**Standing Rules and Orders Adopted by the Legislative Assembly, and Approved
by the Governor**
Together with the joint standing orders of the two houses

ISBN/EAN: 9783744727044

Printed in Europe, USA, Canada, Australia, Japan

Cover: Foto ©Suzi / pixelio.de

More available books at **www.hansebooks.com**

QUEENSLAND.

Legislative Assembly.

STANDING RULES AND ORDERS

ADOPTED BY THE

LEGISLATIVE ASSEMBLY,

AND

APPROVED BY THE GOVERNOR;

TOGETHER WITH THE

JOINT STANDING ORDERS OF THE TWO HOUSES.

BRISBANE:

BY AUTHORITY: JAMES C. BEAL, GOVERNMENT PRINTER.

1892.

CONTENTS.

Chapter.	—	Page.
I.	PROCEEDINGS ON OPENING OF PARLIAMENT: ELECTION OF SPEAKER, AND CHAIRMAN OF COMMITTEES; DEPUTY SPEAKER	5
II.	ORDERLY BEHAVIOUR	9
III.	SITTING AND ADJOURNMENT OF THE HOUSE	9
IV.	MOTIONS ... ...,	11
V.	ORDERS OF THE DAY...	13
VI.	PROCEDURE ON GOVERNMENT DAYS: FORMAL BUSINESS	13
VII.	QUESTIONS TO MEMBERS	14
VIII.	PROCEDURE	14
,,	AMENDMENTS	16
IX.	RULES OF DEBATE	17
X.	DIVISIONS	
XI.	COMMITTEES OF THE WHOLE HOUSE	
XII.	INSTRUCTIONS AND DIRECTIONS TO COMMITTEES OF THE WHOLE HOUSE	
XIII.	SELECT COMMITTEES	27
XIV.	WITNESSES	30
XV.	MESSAGES	32
XVI.	PETITIONS	32
XVII.	PUBLIC BILLS	34
XVIII.	PRIVATE BILLS...	39
XIX.	ACCOUNTS, PAPERS, AND PRINTING	41
XX.	SUPPLY, AND WAYS AND MEANS	41
XXI.	CONTEMPT	43
XXII.	DUTIES OF THE CLERK OF THE ASSEMBLY ..	45
XXIII.	MISCELLANEOUS	46

CONTENTS—*continued*.

RULES OF PRACTICE.

Number.	—	Page.
1	*Members await Message from Commissioners*	5
2	*On receiving Message from Commissioners, Members proceed to Council Chamber*	5
3	*Commissioners for swearing Members*	5
4	*Member proposed as Speaker submits himself to the House*	6
5	*Speaker elect returns acknowledgments and is congratulated*	6
6	*House adjourns after election of Speaker*	6
7	*Speaker elect presents himself for Royal Approbation* ...	6
8	*Speaker lays Claim to Rights and Privileges of the House*	6
9	*Speaker reports the Royal Approbation and Confirmation of Rights and Privileges*	7
10	*House attends Governor in Council Chamber* ...	7
11	*Speaker reports Speech*	8
12	*Use of Benches on either side of the House*	9
13	*House may proceed without Quorum when no notice taken*	11
14	*Vote of Thanks*	12
15	*Member unable to stand may speak sitting*	17
16	*Witnesses not examined on oath except in certain cases* ...	31
17	*Form of Statement of Enacting Authority*	34
18	*Quarrels not to be prosecuted*	44

Chapter.	JOINT STANDING RULES AND ORDERS OF THE LEGISLATIVE COUNCIL AND LEGISLATIVE ASSEMBLY :—	
I.	Messages	47
II.	Bills	49
III.	Practice of Imperial Parliament	50

STANDING RULES AND ORDERS

OF THE

LEGISLATIVE ASSEMBLY

OF

QUEENSLAND.

(Adopted by the Legislative Assembly, 17th August, 1892; and Approved by
His Excellency the Governor, 22nd September, 1892.)

CHAPTER I.—PROCEEDINGS ON OPENING OF PARLIAMENT: ELECTION OF SPEAKER AND CHAIRMAN OF COMMITTEES AND DEPUTY SPEAKER.

PROCLAMATION TO BE READ.

1. On the first day of the meeting of a new Parliament for the
despatch of Business pursuant to the Governor's proclamation,
Members being assembled at the time and place appointed, the Clerk
of the Assembly, or some other person appointed by the Governor in
Council for that purpose, shall read the proclamation.

MEMBERS AWAIT MESSAGE FROM COMMISSIONERS.

1. *The Members await a Message from the Commissioners appointed
by the Governor for opening the Parliament.*

ON RECEIVING MESSAGE FROM COMMISSIONERS, MEMBERS PROCEED TO COUNCIL CHAMBER.

2. *On receiving the Message from the Commissioners for opening
the Parliament, the Members of the Assembly proceed to the Council
Chamber to hear the Commission read.*

COMMISSIONERS FOR SWEARING MEMBERS.

3. *The Assembly being returned into their own House, Commissioners appointed by the Governor for swearing Members produce
their Commission, which is read by the Clerk.*

WRITS FOR GENERAL ELECTION.

2. The writs for a General Election having been previously delivered to the Clerk of the Assembly, the returns endorsed thereon shall be read by the Clerk.

MEMBERS SWORN.

3. Members shall then be sworn as prescribed by the Constitution Act, and shall sign the Roll of Members.

A MEMBER PROPOSED AS SPEAKER.

4. After the Members present have been sworn, a Member, addressing himself to the Clerk, shall propose some Member, then present, to the House, for their Speaker, and move that such Member "Do take the Chair of the House as Speaker," which Motion must be seconded.

WHEN UNOPPOSED, SUCH MEMBER CALLED TO CHAIR.

5. If one Member only is proposed as Speaker, he shall be called to the Chair of this House without Question put.

MEMBER PROPOSED SUBMITS HIMSELF TO THE HOUSE.

4. *The Member on being called to the Chair expresses in his place his sense of the honour proposed to be conferred upon him, and submits himself to the pleasure of the House.*

WHEN ELECTION OF SPEAKER IS OPPOSED.

6. If more than one Member is proposed as Speaker, the Clerk of the Assembly shall, in the order in which the Members have been proposed, put the Question, "That Mr. —— do take the Chair of the House as Speaker"; which shall be resolved in the Affirmative or Negative.

SPEAKER ELECT RETURNS ACKNOWLEDGMENTS AND IS CONGRATULATED.

5. *Having been conducted to the Chair, the Member elected returns his acknowledgments to the House for the honour conferred upon him, and thereupon sits down in the Chair, and a Member offers his congratulations.*

HOUSE TO ADJOURN.

6. *A Member then moves that the House at its rising do adjourn until a future day at an hour to be named, and then that the House do now adjourn.*

THE SPEAKER ELECT PRESENTS HIMSELF FOR ROYAL APPROBATION.

7. *On the next sitting-day, the House being met, Mr. Speaker elect, accompanied by such Members as think fit to attend, presents himself to the Governor for Her Majesty's Royal Approbation.*

SPEAKER LAYS CLAIM TO RIGHTS AND PRIVILEGES OF THE HOUSE.

8. *Mr. Speaker then, in the name and on behalf of the House, lays claim to their undoubted rights and privileges, and prays that the most favourable construction may be put upon all their proceedings.*

SPEAKER REPORTS THE ROYAL APPROBATION AND CONFIRMATION OF RIGHTS AND PRIVILEGES.

9. *Mr. Speaker, being returned, reports that he has attended the Governor and that Her Majesty was pleased, by Her Representative, to approve of the choice the House had made of him to be their Speaker; and that he has, in their name and on their behalf, laid claim to all their undoubted rights and privileges, which Her Majesty, by Her Representative, has confirmed to them in as full and ample manner as they have been heretofore granted or allowed by Her Majesty.*

VACANCY IN OFFICE OF SPEAKER.

7. When a vacancy occurs in the office of Speaker, a new Speaker shall be elected in the same manner as hereinbefore provided.

APPOINTMENT OF CHAIRMAN OF COMMITTEES.—VACANCY.

8. The House shall, by Resolution in each Parliament, appoint a Member to be Chairman of Committees of the whole House.

When a vacancy occurs in the office of Chairman, a new Chairman shall be appointed in like manner.

ABSENCE OF SPEAKER.

9. Whenever the House is informed by the Clerk at the Table of the unavoidable absence of Mr. Speaker at the meeting of the House, the Chairman of Committees, so long as Mr. Speaker is absent, shall perform the duties and exercise the authority of Mr. Speaker in relation to all proceedings of the House as Deputy Speaker, but shall give place to Mr. Speaker on his arrival, and so on from day to day until the House otherwise orders : Provided that if the House adjourns for more than twenty-four hours, the Deputy Speaker shall continue to perform the duties and exercise the authority of Speaker for twenty-four hours only after such Adjournment.

TEMPORARY ABSENCE OF SPEAKER DURING SITTING.

10. When, in consequence of protracted sittings of the House, or from any other cause, Mr. Speaker is unable to continue in the Chair, the Chairman of Committees shall take the Chair as Deputy Speaker during Mr. Speaker's absence.

ABSENCE OF CHAIRMAN.

11. In the absence of the Chairman of Committees, or if he is acting as Deputy Speaker, the House shall appoint another Member to act as Chairman of Committees in his place.

DEPUTY SPEAKER.

12. The House may from time to time appoint another Member to be Deputy Speaker, who shall, in the absence of both Mr. Speaker and the Chairman of Committees, take the Chair as Deputy Speaker.

HOUSE ATTENDS GOVERNOR IN COUNCIL CHAMBER.

10. *On the receipt of a Message to attend the Governor in the Legislative Council Chamber, the Speaker with the House proceeds to the Council Chamber.*

SPEAKER REPORTS SPEECH.

11. *On the return of the House from the Council Chamber, Mr. Speaker reports that the House has this day attended the Governor in the Council Chamber, and that His Excellency was pleased to make a Speech to both Houses of Parliament, of which Speech Mr. Speaker has, for greater accuracy, obtained a copy, which he then reads to the House.*

BILL READ BEFORE SPEECH REPORTED.

13. The Governor's Speech announcing the causes of summoning Parliament shall be reported to the House by Mr. Speaker ; but before such report some Bill may be read the First time without notice.

ADDRESS IN REPLY TO SPEECH.

14. The Speech having been read, a Motion for an Address to the Governor in reply to His Excellency's Speech shall be made and seconded, and the House will resolve to agree to the same with or without Amendments.

ADDRESS PRESENTED BY MR. SPEAKER.

15. The Address in Reply to the Governor's Speech shall be presented to the Governor by Mr. Speaker, accompanied by such Members of the Assembly as think fit to attend with him.

SUPPLY.

16. After the Address in Reply has been agreed to, the Governor's Speech shall be ordered to be taken into consideration at the next sitting of the House. The House at the appointed day shall proceed to take the Speech into consideration, and so much of it as was addressed to the Assembly shall be again read by Mr. Speaker ; and a Motion shall be made that the House will on a future day resolve itself into a Committee of the Whole to consider the Supply to be granted to Her Majesty.

ADDRESSES TO GOVERNOR: HOW PRESENTED.

17. Addresses to the Governor shall be presented by Mr. Speaker, unless otherwise ordered.

GOVERNOR'S ANSWER TO BE REPORTED. ·

18. The Governor's answer to an Address shall be reported by Mr. Speaker to the House.

INTRODUCTION OF NEW MEMBERS.

19. Members returned, not having been elected at a General Election, shall be introduced by a Member, and shall then be sworn and shall sign the Roll of Members. A Member may be introduced at any time, but not so as to interrupt Mr. Speaker or a Member who is addressing the House, nor after a Division has been called for.

CHAPTER II.—ORDERLY BEHAVIOUR.

ENTERING AND LEAVING THE HOUSE.

20. A Member is to be uncovered when he enters or leaves the House, or moves to any other part of the House, and shall make obeisance to the Chair in entering and leaving the House.

MEMBERS LEAVING THEIR SEATS.

21. A Member shall not pass between the Chair and a Member who is speaking; nor between the Chair and the Table.

ENTERING THE HOUSE.

22. A Member when he comes into the House shall take his place, and shall not stand in any of the passages or gangways.

USE OF BENCHES ON EITHER SIDE OF THE HOUSE.

12. *The front bench on the right hand of the Chair is reserved for Members holding office under the Crown, and the front bench on the left hand of the Chair, and the front cross-benches on either side of the Chair, are ordinarily occupied by Members who have held office under the Crown.*

CHAPTER III.—SITTING AND ADJOURNMENT OF THE HOUSE.

DAYS OF MEETING.

23. The House shall from time to time appoint the days and the hour of each day on which it will meet for the despatch of Business.

IF QUORUM NOT PRESENT WITHIN HALF-AN-HOUR, HOUSE TO STAND ADJOURNED.

24. Mr. Speaker shall take the Chair as soon after the time appointed for the meeting of the House as a quorum of Members is present; but the House will not proceed to Business until half-an-hour after the time so appointed. If at the expiration of half-an-hour after the time appointed a quorum is not present, Mr. Speaker shall without taking the Chair adjourn the House to the next sitting-day.

WHEN NO QUORUM AFTER BUSINESS.

25. At any time after the House has proceeded to Business, if it appears on notice being taken by any Member, or on the report by the Tellers of a Division, that a quorum is not present, Mr. Speaker shall adjourn the House, without Question put, to the next sitting-day.

QUORUM OF COMMITTEE OF THE WHOLE HOUSE.

26. The same number of Members shall be required to form a quorum in Committee of the whole House as are required to form a quorum of the House.

WHEN CHAIRMAN OF COMMITTEES REPORTS THAT A QUORUM OF MEMBERS IS NOT PRESENT.

27. If the Chairman of a Committee of the whole House reports to the House that a quorum of Members is not present, Mr. Speaker shall count the House, and if a quorum is not present, he shall adjourn the House, without Question put, to the next sitting-day.

ADJOURNMENT BEFORE NEXT SITTING-DAY FIXED.

28. If the House stands adjourned on any day before the days and hours of sitting have been appointed by the House, it shall stand adjourned to the next following day, not being a Sunday, at the same hour on which it was appointed to meet on the day on which it so stands adjourned.

MEMBER TAKING NOTICE OF WANT OF QUORUM SHALL BE COUNTED.

29. A Member who calls the attention of Mr. Speaker, or of the Chairman of Committees, to the fact that there is not a quorum of Members present, shall be held to be present during the counting of the House.

BEFORE COUNTING, BELL TO BE RUNG.

30. The Division Bell shall be rung and kept ringing for two minutes before Mr. Speaker proceeds to count the House, and the doors shall be kept unlocked.

HOUSE ADJOURNED ON ITS OWN RESOLUTION.

31. Except when Mr. Speaker adjourns the House in consequence of a quorum not being present, the House shall be adjourned only by its own Resolution.

BUSINESS NOT DISPOSED OF AT ADJOURNMENT.

32. Notices of Motion and Orders of the Day not disposed of at the time of the Adjournment of the House shall, on the next sitting-day, take precedence in the order of the days for which they were first given or appointed, but so as not to displace on any day Notices of Motion or Orders given or appointed for that day.

Business which is under discussion at the time of an Adjournment for want of a quorum, or which stands adjourned without Question put under an Order of the House giving precedence to other Business at an hour at which such Business is under discussion, shall stand as an Order of the Day for the next sitting-day under the foregoing provisions of this Order.

Business otherwise superseded after it has been entered upon shall lapse.

PRIVATE NOTICES OF MOTION AND ORDERS OF THE DAY TAKE PRECEDENCE ALTERNATELY.

33. Except on days on which Government Business is appointed to take precedence, Notices of Motion and Orders of the Day, not being Government Business, shall respectively, unless otherwise ordered, have precedence on alternate sitting-days of the House; but so that if there are two days in a week in which Government Business has not precedence the relative order of precedence of Notices of Motion and Orders of the Day on such days in the following week shall be reversed.

But Notices of Motion relating to the Business of the House shall take precedence of all other Business.

When Notices of Motion or Orders of the Day, not being Government Business, are given or appointed for a day on which Government Business has not precedence, and the House is afterwards adjourned over that day, or a quorum is not present on that day, such Notices of Motion and Orders of the Day shall, on the next day on which the House sits, not being a day on which Government Business has precedence, take precedence in the Order of the days for which they were first given or appointed, but so as not to displace on any day Notices of Motion or Orders given or appointed for that day.

HOUSE MAY PROCEED WITHOUT QUORUM WHEN NO NOTICE TAKEN.

13. *The House proceeds with Business, although less than a quorum be present, until notice is taken thereof.*

CHAPTER IV.—MOTIONS.

FAIR COPY OF NOTICE OF MOTION TO BE DELIVERED.

34. A Member giving Notice of a Motion shall read it aloud, and shall deliver to the Clerk at the Table a copy of the Notice, fairly written or printed, together with his name and the day on which he proposes to bring it forward.

NOT TO BE GIVEN FOR SAME DAY, OR MORE THAN EIGHT DAYS IN ADVANCE.

35. A Notice of a Motion may not be given for the same day on which it is given, nor for a day later than the eighth next sitting-day of the House.

NOTICE BY PROXY.

36. A Member may give Notice of a Motion for another Member.

TO BE PRINTED WITH VOTES.

37. Notices of Motion shall be printed and circulated with the Votes and Proceedings.

TERMS MAY BE ALTERED.

38. After a Notice of a Motion has been given, the terms thereof may be altered by the Member on delivering at the Table an amended Notice, at least one day before the day for which the Notice is given.

MAY NOT BE ANTICIPATED.

39. A Member, having given Notice of a Motion for a certain day, may give fresh Notice for a later but not for an earlier day.

NOT TO BE GIVEN AFTER HOUSE HAS PROCEEDED TO ORDERS OF THE DAY.

40. A Notice of a Motion shall not be received after the House has proceeded to the Orders of the Day, unless with the leave of the House.

ORDER ON BUSINESS PAPER.

41. Notices of Motion, when first given, shall be set down on the Business Paper in the order in which they have been given.

QUESTIONS OF PRIVILEGE.

42. An urgent Motion, directly concerning the Privileges of the House, shall take precedence of other Motions as well as of Orders of the Day.

NOTICES MAY BE EXPUNGED.

43. A Notice containing unbecoming expressions may be expunged from the Business Paper by order of the House.

VOTE OF THANKS.

14. *Precedence is ordinarily given by courtesy to a Motion for a Vote of Thanks of the House.*

NOTICE OF MOTION NECESSARY.

44. A Member shall not make any Motion, initiating a subject for discussion, except in pursuance of Notice or by leave of the House.

PRINTING OF PAPERS WITHOUT NOTICE.

45. Motions for the printing of Papers which are presented by command of the Governor, or in answer to an Address, or in compliance with an Order of the House or of a Select Committee, or pursuant to a Statute, may be made without Notice by the Member presenting them on the presentation of such Papers.

ORDER OF MOTIONS.

46. Motions shall take precedence of Orders of the Day, except on those days on which Orders of the Day have precedence, and the Members who have given Notices of Motion shall be called upon to make the Motions in the order in which the Notices stand on the Business Paper. If a Motion is not made, it shall lapse.

MOTIONS BY LEAVE.

47. A Motion may be made by leave of the House without Notice.

NOT SECONDED.

48. A Motion not seconded shall lapse, unless it relates to an Order of the Day, or is made in Committee of the Whole House.

WITHDRAWN.

49. A Member who has made a Motion may withdraw the same by leave of the House.

MOTIONS WITHDRAWN MAY BE MADE AGAIN.

50. A Motion which has been withdrawn by leave of the House may be made again in the same Session.

NOT TO BE WITHDRAWN IN ABSENCE OF PROPOSER.

51. A Motion or Amendment shall not be withdrawn in the absence of the Member who proposed it.

AMENDMENT WITHDRAWN, ETC., BEFORE ORIGINAL MOTION.

52. When an Amendment has been proposed to a Motion, the original Motion shall not be withdrawn until the Amendment has been withdrawn or negatived.

CHAPTER V.—ORDERS OF THE DAY.

DEFINITION.

53. An Order of the Day is a Bill or other matter which the House has ordered to be taken into consideration, or done, on a particular day.

ROTATION.

54. The Orders of the Day shall be disposed of in the order in which they stand upon the Business Paper.

TO BE READ WITHOUT QUESTION PUT.

55. Mr. Speaker shall direct the Clerk to read the Orders of the Day, without any Question first put.

NEED NOT BE SECONDED.

56. An Order of the Day may be moved without being seconded.

LAPSED ORDERS MAY BE RESTORED.

57. A lapsed Order of the Day may be restored to the Business Paper by order of the House.

CHAPTER VI.—PROCEDURE ON GOVERNMENT DAYS: FORMAL BUSINESS.

ORDER OF BUSINESS ON GOVERNMENT DAYS.

58. The right is reserved to Her Majesty's Ministers to place any Notices of Motion or Orders of the Day, whether relating to Government Business or not, upon the Business Paper in the rotation in which they desire them to be taken, on any days on which Government Business has precedence.

FORMAL OR UNOPPOSED BUSINESS.

59. Before the House proceeds to the Notices of Motion or Orders of the Day, Mr. Speaker shall inquire from the Chair with respect to each Motion of which Notice has been given for the day, and each Order of the Day for the Third reading of a Bill, whether there is any objection to its being taken as a Formal Motion or Order: And if, upon such inquiry being made from the Chair, no objection is taken by any Member, the Motion or Order shall be deemed to be a Formal Motion or Order.

TO TAKE PRECEDENCE.

60. Formal Motions and Orders shall take precedence of all other Motions and Orders of the Day, and shall be disposed of in the relative order in which they stand on the Business Paper.

NO AMENDMENT OR DEBATE ALLOWED.

61. No Amendment or Debate shall be allowed on a Formal Motion or Order of the Day, or upon the further proceedings following the Third reading of a Bill which is a Formal Order, but the House may proceed to Division thereon as in other cases.

NOT TO PREVENT OTHER BUSINESS.

62. The disposal of Formal Motions and Orders shall not prevent any Business from being done which is required to be done before the House proceeds to the Notices of Motion or Orders of the Day.

CHAPTER VII.—QUESTIONS TO MEMBERS.

QUESTIONS TO MEMBERS.

63. At the time appointed for giving Notices of Motion a Member may put any Question of which Notice has been given to any other Member of the House relating to any Bill, Motion, or other public matter connected with the Business of the House.

NO DEBATE ON PUTTING QUESTIONS.

64. In putting a Question, no argument or opinion shall be offered, nor any fact stated, except so far as is necessary to explain the Question.

NOR ON ANSWERING.

65. In answering a Question, a Member shall not debate the matter to which the Question refers.

CHAPTER VIII.—PROCEDURE.

QUESTION PROPOSED.

66. When a Motion has been made and seconded, a Question thereupon shall be proposed to the House by Mr. Speaker.

IRREGULAR, NOT PROPOSED.

67. If a Motion or Amendment is irregular, or out of Order, no Question shall be proposed thereupon by Mr. Speaker.

QUESTION PUT, AND, IF NOT HEARD, AGAIN STATED.

68. A Debate being closed, Mr. Speaker shall put the Question to the House, and, if the same is not heard, shall again state it.

DETERMINED BY MAJORITY OF VOICES.

69. A Question being put, shall be resolved by the majority of voices—Aye or No.

SPEAKER DECLARES MAJORITY.

70. Mr. Speaker shall state whether in his opinion the Ayes or Noes have it; but if his opinion is not agreed to by any Member the Question shall be determined by a Division.

SAME QUESTION NOT TO BE AGAIN PROPOSED.

71. A Question or Amendment shall not be proposed which is the same in substance as any Question which, during the same Session, has been resolved in the Affirmative or Negative.

QUESTION DIVIDED.

72. The House may order a complicated Question to be divided.

QUESTION SUPERSEDED.

73. A Question may be superseded, 1. By the Adjournment of the House on the Motion of a Member; 2. By a Resolution of the House to pass to some other Business; 3. By Amendments; 4. By the Previous Question, "That this Question be not now put," being resolved in the Affirmative.

PREVIOUS QUESTION PRECLUDES AMENDMENT.

74. The Previous Question having been proposed, an Amendment of the Main Question shall not be entertained unless the Previous Question has been withdrawn.

PREVIOUS QUESTION NEGATIVED.

75. The Previous Question having been resolved in the Negative, the Main Question shall be at once put, without Amendment or further Debate.

NOT TO BE AMENDED, BUT MAY BE SUPERSEDED BY ADJOURNMENT.

76. No Amendment shall be offered to the Previous Question, but such Question may be superseded by the Adjournment of the House.

NOT TO BE MOVED UPON AMENDMENT.

77. The Previous Question shall not be moved upon an Amendment.

DEBATE UPON PREVIOUS QUESTION MAY BE ADJOURNED.

78. A Debate upon the Previous Question may be adjourned.

WHEN PREVIOUS QUESTION NOT TO BE MOVED.

79. A Motion to pass to some other Business having been made and negatived, a Motion for the Previous Question shall not be entertained.

WHEN PREVIOUS QUESTION PROPOSED ON SERIES OF RESOLUTIONS.

80. Whenever the Previous Question is proposed upon a Question consisting of a series of Resolutions, which have been brought under discussion or Debate as one Motion, the decision of the Previous Question before putting the Question on the first of such Resolutions shall be conclusive, whether in the Affirmative or Negative, as regards the whole of such Resolutions.

VOTES MAY BE RESCINDED.

81. A Resolution or other Order of the House may be read and rescinded; but not on the same day as that on which it was passed. A Motion for rescission must be made by a Member who voted for the Resolution or Order proposed to be rescinded.

ORDER DISCHARGED.

82. An Order of the House may be read and discharged.

AMENDMENTS.

FORMS OF AMENDMENT.

83. A Question having been proposed, may be amended by omitting certain words only, by omitting certain words in order to insert or add other words, or by inserting or adding words.

AMENDMENTS TO BE SECONDED.

84. An Amendment proposed but not seconded shall not be entertained by the House.

AMENDMENT TO OMIT WORDS.

85. When the proposed Amendment is to omit words, Mr. Speaker shall put a Question, "That the words proposed to be omitted stand part of the Question," which shall be resolved by the House in the Affirmative or Negative.

TO SUBSTITUTE WORDS.

86. When the proposed Amendment is to omit words in order to insert or add other words, Mr. Speaker shall put a Question, "That the words proposed to be omitted stand part of the Question"; which if resolved in the Affirmative will dispose of the Amendment; but if in the Negative, another Question shall be put, "That the words (of the Amendment) be inserted" or "added," which shall be resolved in the Affirmative or Negative.

TO INSERT OR ADD WORDS.

87. When the proposed Amendment is to insert or add words, Mr. Speaker shall put a Question, "That such words be inserted" or "added"; which shall be resolved in the Affirmative or Negative.

NO AMENDMENT WHEN LATER PART OF QUESTION AMENDED.

88. An Amendment may not be proposed in any part of a Question after a later part has been amended, or has been proposed to be amended, unless the proposed Amendment has been withdrawn by leave of the House.

NOR TO WORDS ALREADY AGREED TO.

89. An Amendment shall not be made to any words which the House has ordered to stand part of a Question, except by adding other words thereto. But such an addition shall not be made in Questions relating to the several stages of Bills.

AMENDMENTS MAY BE WITHDRAWN.

90. A proposed Amendment may, by leave of the House, be withdrawn.

ORIGINAL QUESTION PUT.

91. When Amendments have been proposed but not agreed to, the Question shall be put as originally proposed.

QUESTION, AS AMENDED, PUT.

92. When Amendments have been made, the Main Question, as amended, shall be put.

ORDER IN WHICH AMENDMENTS TO BE PUT.

93. When several Amendments have been proposed to be made to a Question, they shall be put singly, in the order in which, if agreed to, they would stand in the amended Question.

WHEN AMENDMENT MOVED, ORIGINAL MOTION CANNOT BE VARIED.

94. When a Member has made a Motion to which an Amendment is moved, he shall not substitute another Motion unless the Amendment to the original Motion has been withdrawn.

AMENDMENTS TO AMENDMENTS.

95. Amendments may be proposed to a proposed Amendment whenever it comes to a Question whether the House shall agree to such proposed Amendment.

AMENDMENT DEALT WITH AS IF MAIN QUESTION.

96. Where the original Amendment is either simply to insert, add, or omit words, an Amendment may at once be proposed to it without reference to the Main Question, which will be dealt with when the Amendments have been disposed of.

AMENDMENT TO ORDER OF THE DAY.

97. An Amendment to a Question relating to an Order of the Day must be relevant to such Question.

"NOW ADJOURN"—NO AMENDMENT.

98. No Amendment shall be moved to the Question, " That this House do now adjourn."

CHAPTER IX.—RULES OF DEBATE.

MEMBERS TO ADDRESS MR. SPEAKER.

99. Every Member desiring to speak shall rise in his place uncovered, and address himself to Mr. Speaker.

MEMBER UNABLE TO STAND MAY SPEAK SITTING.

15. *By the special indulgence of the House, a Member unable conveniently to stand, by reason of sickness or infirmity, is permitted to speak sitting and uncovered.*

NO SPEAKING AFTER VOICES GIVEN.

100. A Member may not speak to a Question, after it has been put by Mr. Speaker, and the Voices have been given in the Affirmative and Negative thereon.

SPEAKER TO CALL UPON MEMBER TO SPEAK.

101. When two or more Members rise to speak, Mr. Speaker shall call upon the Member who first rose in his place.

MOTION THAT MEMBER BE HEARD, ETC.

102. A Motion may be made that a Member who has risen " be now heard "; or that a Member who is speaking " be not heard " or " be not further heard."

B

WHEN MEMBER MAY SPEAK.

103. A Member may speak to any Question before the House, or upon a Question or Amendment to be proposed by himself, or upon a Question of Order arising out of the Debate, but not otherwise.

PERSONAL EXPLANATION WHEN NO QUESTION.

104. By the indulgence of the House a Member may explain matters of a personal nature, although there is no Question before the House; but such matters may not be debated.

WHEN ALREADY SPOKEN.

105. A Member who has spoken to a Question may be heard to explain himself in regard to some material part of his speech, but shall not introduce any new matter.

MEMBERS NOT TO SPEAK TWICE.

106. A Member shall not speak twice to the same Question, except in explanation, or in Committee of the whole House.

REPLY, WHEN ALLOWED.

107. A reply shall be allowed to a Member who has made a substantive Motion or moved an Order of the Day; but not to a Member who has moved an Amendment, an Instruction to a Committee, or the Previous Question, or the Adjournment of the House to supersede a Question, or has moved that the House do pass to some other Business.

MEMBER NOT TO INTERRUPT ANOTHER.

108. A Member shall not interrupt another while addressing the House, except by leave of such other Member, or of the House, and for the purpose of making a personal explanation.

SPEAKING TO ORDER OR PRIVILEGE.

109. A Member may rise to speak to Order, or upon a matter of Privilege suddenly arising.

QUESTION OF ORDER, HOW DEALT WITH.

110. Upon a Question of Order being raised the Member called to Order shall resume his seat; and after the Question of Order has been stated to Mr. Speaker by the Member rising to the Question of Order, Mr. Speaker shall give his opinion thereon : but may first invite the opinion of the House. But it shall be competent for any Member to take the sense of the House after Mr. Speaker has given his opinion, and in that case any Member may address the House upon the Question.

OFFENSIVE WORDS AGAINST MEMBER.

111. A Member shall not use unbecoming or offensive words in reference to another Member of the House.

DIGRESSIONS, REFERENCE TO PREVIOUS DEBATE, PERSONAL REFLECTIONS, ETC.

112. A Member shall not digress from the subject-matter under discussion, or comment upon expressions used by another Member in a previous Debate of the same Session; and all imputations of improper motives, and all personal reflections, shall be deemed highly disorderly.

WORDS TAKEN DOWN IN THE HOUSE.

113. When a Member objects to words used in Debate, and, stating them, desires them to be taken down, Mr. Speaker, if it appears to be the pleasure of the House, shall direct them to be taken down by the Clerk accordingly.

IN COMMITTEE.

114. In a Committee of the whole House the Chairman, if it appears to be the pleasure of the Committee, shall direct words objected to, and stated by the Member objecting, to be taken down in order that they may be reported to the House.

OBJECTION TO BE TAKEN AT THE TIME.

115. Every such objection shall be taken at the time when the words are used, and not after another Member has spoken.

MEMBER NOT EXPLAINING OR RETRACTING.

116. A Member having used objectionable words, and not explaining or retracting the same, or offering apologies for the use thereof to the satisfaction of the House, shall be censured by Mr. Speaker, and may be suspended from the service of the House for such period as the House may think fit.

NO DISTURBANCE WHILE MEMBER SPEAKING; OFFENDING MEMBER SUSPENDED.

117. A Member shall not make any noise or disturbance whilst any Member is orderly debating, or whilst a Bill, Order, or other matter, is being read or opened; and, in case such noise or disturbance is made and persisted in after warning from Mr. Speaker, Mr. Speaker shall call by name upon the Member making the same, and every such Member will incur the displeasure and censure of the House, and may be suspended from the service of the House for such period as the House may think fit.

DISORDER IN COMMITTEE TO BE REPORTED TO HOUSE.

118. Order shall be maintained in the House by Mr. Speaker and in a Committee of the Whole House by the Chairman; if any disorder arises in Committee, the Chairman shall report the same to the House.

WHEN SPEAKER OR CHAIRMAN RISES, MEMBER SPEAKING TO SIT DOWN.

119. Whenever Mr. Speaker or the Chairman rises to speak during a Debate, any Member then speaking or offering to speak shall sit down, and Mr. Speaker or the Chairman shall be heard without interruption.

MEMBER TO WITHDRAW WHILE CONDUCT UNDER CONSIDERATION.

120. A Member against whom a charge has been made, having been heard in his place, shall withdraw while the charge is under consideration.

ADJOURNMENT OF DEBATE.

121. A Debate may be adjourned to a later hour on the same day, or to any other day.

DEBATE BEING RESUMED, MEMBERS NOT TO SPEAK AGAIN.

122. When a Debate has been adjourned, a Member who has spoken to the Question may not speak again to the same Question when the Debate is resumed.

MAY SPEAK AGAIN TO NEW QUESTION.

123. A Member who has spoken to a Question may speak again to the Question of Adjournment, or to any other new Question which may arise.

HAVING SPOKEN TO ADJOURNMENT, MAY SPEAK TO MAIN QUESTION.

124. A Member who has spoken only on the Question of Adjournment may speak subsequently on the Main Question.

MAIN QUESTION NOT TO BE ENTERED UPON ON QUESTION OF ADJOURNMENT.

125. A Member may not enter upon the Main Question when speaking to the Question of Adjournment.

MEMBER WHO HAS SPOKEN MAY NOT MAKE MOTION, BUT MAY SPEAK TO NEW MOTION.

126. A Member who has spoken may not move an Amendment, or the Adjournment of the House, or the Adjournment of the Debate, or any similar matter, but he may speak on any such Motion when it is made by another Member.

SAME MEMBER NOT TO MOVE ADJOURNMENT OF HOUSE AND DEBATE.

127. A Member who has moved or seconded the Adjournment of the House may not afterwards move or second the Adjournment of the Debate, or *vice versâ*.

ADJOURNMENT BEING NEGATIVED, NOT TO BE PROPOSED AGAIN IMMEDIATELY.

128. If a Motion for the Adjournment of the House or of the Debate has been negatived, it shall not be proposed again, without the leave of the House, until some other Question has intervened.

NO REFERENCE TO PROCEEDINGS OF COMMITTEES UNTIL REPORTED.

129. Reference shall not be made to any proceedings of a Committee of the Whole House, or of a Select Committee, until the same have been reported to the House.

NO MOTION FOR ADJOURNMENT OF THE HOUSE EXCEPT IN CERTAIN CASES.

130. A Motion for the Adjournment of the House, other than the usual Motion to terminate the sitting of the House at the end of the Business of the Day, shall not be entertained, except for the purpose of debating a definite matter of urgent public importance, the subject of which has been first stated to Mr. Speaker in writing.

Any such Motion shall be proposed by the Mover without Debate in the first instance, but shall not be put by Mr. Speaker unless five other Members at least rise in their places to support it.

If five Members so rise in their places the Mover may proceed, but may not speak for more than thirty minutes to debate the Motion, and any other Member debating the Motion, or the Mover speaking in reply, may not speak for more than twenty minutes, and every Member making or debating any such Motion shall confine himself to the single matter in respect of which the Motion is made.

In the Debate on a Motion for Adjournment reference may be made to facts disclosed in answers to Questions put to Members either on the same day or on a previous day.

NO SECOND MOTION FOR ADJOURNMENT ON SAME DAY.

131. A second Motion for the Adjournment of the House, other than the usual Motion to terminate the sitting of the House at the end of the Business of the day, shall not be made on the same day, except by the consent of the House obtained by Mr. Speaker without Debate.

NO AMENDMENT ON GOING INTO COMMITTEE OF SUPPLY OR WAYS AND MEANS WITHOUT LEAVE OF HOUSE.

132. On the Order of the Day for the House to resolve itself into Committee of Supply or Ways and Means an Amendment or contingent Motion shall not be entertained without the leave of the House, and no Debate shall be allowed upon the Motion for such leave, except a statement of the subject-matter of the intended Amendment or Motion, in making which the Mover may not debate the same for more than ten minutes.

NO MOTION OF AN OBSTRUCTIVE CHARACTER THAT CHAIRMAN LEAVE CHAIR ALLOWED.

133. In Committee of Supply or Ways and Means, or in a Committee of the whole House on a Bill or Resolution, a Member shall not make any Motion for the Chairman to leave the Chair, which by the ruling of the Chairman without Debate is held to be of an obstructive character or not consistent with the regular and orderly conduct of the Business of the Committee.

SPEAKER OR CHAIRMAN MAY CALL ATTENTION TO IRRELEVANCE AND ORDER DISCONTINUANCE OF SPEECH.

134. Mr. Speaker, or, in a Committee of the whole House, the Chairman, may call the attention of the House or the Committee, as the case may be, to continued irrelevance or tedious repetition on the part of a Member, and may after such warning direct the Member to discontinue his speech : Provided that the Member so directed may require Mr. Speaker or the Chairman, as the case may be, to put the Question that he be further heard, and such Question, if so required to be put, shall be put without Debate.

MOTION MAY BE MADE "THAT QUESTION BE NOW PUT."

135. At any time during a Debate in the House or during the proceedings of a Committee of the whole House, and whether a Member is speaking or not, any Member may move "That the Question be now put"; and, if Mr. Speaker or the Chairman is of opinion that the Question has been sufficiently debated, such Motion shall be put

forthwith without Debate, but shall not pass in the Affirmative unless two-thirds of the Members present, being at least one-third of the whole number of the Members of the House, give their votes for the Motion; and if the Motion is carried, Mr. Speaker or the Chairman shall forthwith put the Question to the vote.

RIGHT OF REPLY.

136. When the House or a Committee of the whole House has directed that a Question "be now put," the Mover, proposer, or introducer of the Question shall, if otherwise entitled to reply, be permitted to speak in reply before the Question is put, but shall not in such reply debate the matter in the House for more than thirty minutes, or in a Committee of the whole House for more than fifteen minutes.

CHAPTER X.—DIVISIONS.

SERGEANT-AT-ARMS TO RING A BELL, AND SANDGLASS TO BE TURNED.

137. When a Division is demanded, the Sergeant-at-Arms shall ring a bell, and a two-minute sandglass, to be kept on the Table for that purpose, shall be turned ; and the doors shall not be closed until after the lapse of two minutes, as indicated by such sandglass.

DOORS CLOSED AFTER THE LAPSE OF TWO MINUTES.

138. Immediately after the lapse of such period of two minutes Mr. Speaker shall direct the doors to be closed, and no Member shall then enter or leave the House until after the Division is reported.

NO MEMBER MAY VOTE UNLESS PRESENT WHEN QUESTION IS PUT.

139. A Member shall not be entitled to vote in a Division unless he is present in the House when the Question is put with the doors closed; and the vote of any Member not so present will be disallowed.

EVERY MEMBER THEN PRESENT MUST VOTE.

140. Every Member present in the House when the Question is put shall vote.

WHEN QUESTION PUT, "AYES" AND "NOES" SHALL TAKE DIFFERENT SIDES OF THE HOUSE.

141. When the doors have been closed Mr. Speaker shall again put the Question, and after the voices have been given, shall declare whether, in his opinion, the "Ayes" or the "Noes" have it; which not being agreed to, the "Ayes" shall take their places on the right side of the House, and the "Noes" on the left side of the House, and Mr. Speaker shall appoint Tellers, two from each side.

A Member may not move from his place after the Tellers have been appointed.

IF NOT TWO TELLERS, NO DIVISION.

142. In case there are not two Tellers on one side, Mr. Speaker shall forthwith declare the Resolution of the House.

DIVISION LISTS ENTERED IN THE VOTES.

143. An entry of the lists of Divisions in the House and in Committees of the whole House, shall be made in the Votes and Proceedings.

TELLERS REPORT THE NUMBERS.

144. The Tellers shall report the numbers to Mr. Speaker, who shall declare them to the House.

IN CASE OF CONFUSION OR ERROR, HOUSE AGAIN DIVIDES.

145. In case of confusion or error concerning the numbers reported, unless the same can be otherwise corrected, the House shall proceed to another Division.

MISTAKES CORRECTED IN VOTES AND PROCEEDINGS.

146. If the numbers have been inaccurately reported, the House, on being afterwards informed thereof, will order the Votes and Proceedings to be corrected.

WHEN VOTES ARE EQUAL MR. SPEAKER GIVES CASTING VOTE.

147. In case of an equality of votes upon a Division in the House, Mr. Speaker shall give a casting vote, and any reasons stated by him shall be entered in the Votes and Proceedings.

DIVISION DEMANDED ONLY BY MINORITY.

148. A Division shall be called for only by a Member who has given his voice against the majority as declared by Mr. Speaker.

MEMBERS HAVING GIVEN VOICES, NOT TO VOTE DIFFERENTLY ON DIVISION.

149. A Member, having given his voice with the Ayes or Noes, shall not, on a Division being taken, be at liberty to vote with the opposite party; and if he should do so, Mr. Speaker, on being informed thereof, shall order the Division List to be corrected.

DIVISIONS IN COMMITTEE.

150. Divisions in Committee of the whole House shall be taken and recorded in the same manner, and the same rules shall be applicable thereto, as in the case of Divisions in the House itself.

QUESTION OF ORDER DURING DIVISION.

151. A Member, when proposing a Question of Order for the decision of Mr. Speaker or the Chairman of Committees during a Division, shall remain sitting.

NO MEMBER PECUNIARILY INTERESTED MAY VOTE.

152. A Member shall not be entitled to vote either in the House or in a Committee upon any Question in which he has a direct pecuniary interest, and the vote of any Member so interested shall be disallowed.

CHAPTER XI.—COMMITTEES OF THE WHOLE HOUSE.

HOUSE RESOLVES ITSELF INTO COMMITTEE.

153. A Committee of the whole House is appointed by a Resolution, "That this House will resolve itself into a Committee of the whole House " for a purpose specified in the Resolution, or "That a Bill or Resolution be considered in a Committee of the whole House."

SPEAKER LEAVES CHAIR.

154. When such a Resolution has been agreed to, or an Order of the Day read for the House to resolve itself into Committee, Mr. Speaker shall put a Question, "That I do now leave the Chair," which being agreed to, he shall leave the Chair accordingly, and the Chairman shall take the Chair of the Committee at the Table.

COMMITTEE MAY BE PUT OFF TO ANY TIME.

155. Amendments may be moved to the Question for Mr. Speaker to leave the Chair, by omitting all the words after the word "That," in order to add the words "this House will on this day Three months (or Six months, or any other time) resolve itself into the said Committee."

WHEN COMMITTEE HAS REPORTED PROGRESS.

156. When a Bill or other matter (except in the case of Committees of Supply or Ways and Means) has been partly considered in Committee, and progress has been reported, and the House has ordered that the Committee shall sit again on a particular day, Mr. Speaker, when the Order for the Committee has been read, shall forthwith leave the Chair without putting any Question, and the House will thereupon resolve itself into such Committee.

COMMITTEE NOT TO CONSIDER MATTERS NOT REFERRED.

157. The Committee shall consider such matters only as have been referred to it by the House.

QUESTIONS TO BE DECIDED BY MAJORITY, NOT INCLUDING CHAIRMAN.

158. All Questions which arise in a Committee of the whole House shall be decided by the votes of the majority of the Members present, not including the Chairman, and in case of an equality of votes the Chairman shall have a casting vote.

MOTIONS NEED NOT BE SECONDED.

159. A Motion or Amendment made in Committee need not be seconded.

PREVIOUS QUESTION NOT TO BE MOVED.

160. A Motion for the Previous Question shall not be made in Committee.

RULES OF DEBATE SAME AS IN HOUSE.

161. The same order in Debate shall be observed in Committee as in the House.

MEMBERS MAY SPEAK MORE THAN ONCE.

162. In Committee Members may speak more than once to the same Question.

GREATER OR LESSER SUM, LONGER OR SHORTER TIME.

163. When a blank is to be filled up, and there comes a Question between a greater and lesser sum, or between a longer and shorter time, the least sum and the longest time shall first be put to the Question.

SPEAKER TO RESUME CHAIR IN CERTAIN CASES.

164. If any sudden disorder arises in Committee, or a Message from His Excellency the Governor is announced, or the time is come for doing anything which the House has ordered to be done at a stated time, Mr. Speaker shall resume the Chair without any Question being put.

In either of the two former cases, when the matter has been disposed of, the House shall again resolve itself into the Committee without Question put.

MEMBER NOT EXPLAINING OR RETRACTING.

165. If a Member, having used objectionable words, does not explain or retract the same, or offer apologies for the use thereof, to the satisfaction of the Committee, the Chairman shall report his conduct to the House ; and such Member will incur the displeasure and censure of the House, and may be suspended from the service of the House for such period as the House may think fit.

DISTURBANCE BY MEMBERS.

166. A Member shall not make any noise or disturbance while a Member is orderly debating or whilst any matter is under consideration, and, in case such noise or disturbance is made and persisted in after warning from the Chairman, the Chairman shall call by name upon the Member making the same, and, if he does not immediately desist, shall report his conduct to the House, and such Member will incur the displeasure and censure of the House, and may be suspended from the service of the House for such period as the House may think fit.

When the matter so reported has been disposed of, the House shall again resolve itself into the Committee without Question put.

IF WANT OF QUORUM NOTICED, CHAIRMAN LEAVES CHAIR.

167. If at any time during the sitting of a Committee of the whole House notice is taken that a quorum of Members is not present, the Chairman shall, after the bell has been rung as in a Division, forthwith count the Committee, and if a quorum of Members is not present, the Chairman shall leave the Chair and Mr. Speaker shall resume the Chair, and the Chairman shall report the matter to the House.

WHEN A QUORUM OF MEMBERS NOT PRESENT ON DIVISION.

168. If it appears upon a Division in a Committee of the whole House that a quorum of Members is not present, the Chairman shall leave the Chair and Mr. Speaker shall resume the Chair, and the Chairman shall report the matter to the House.

DUTY OF SPEAKER WHEN CHAIRMAN REPORTS THAT A QUORUM OF MEMBERS IS NOT PRESENT.

169. When the Chairman reports to the House that a quorum of Members is not present, Mr. Speaker shall count the House, and if a quorum is not then present, he shall adjourn the House, without Question put, till the next sitting day.

IF QUORUM PRESENT WHEN HOUSE COUNTED BY MR. SPEAKER.

170. If a quorum of Members is present when the House is counted by Mr. Speaker, the House shall again resolve itself into the Committee without Question put.

DEPUTY CHAIRMAN.

171. When, in consequence of the illness of the Chairman, or the protracted sittings of the Committee, or for any other reason, the Chairman is unable to continue in the Chair, he may call upon any Member then present to take the Chair, and the Member so called on shall take the Chair, and shall, until the return of the Chairman, have and exercise all the powers and functions of the Chairman.

REPORT.

172. After all the matters referred to the Committee have been considered, the Chairman shall be directed to report the same to the House.

REPORT OF PROGRESS.

173. When all such matters have not been considered, the Chairman shall be directed to report progress and ask leave to sit again.

MOTION TO LEAVE THE CHAIR.

174. A Motion that the Chairman do now leave the Chair shall, if carried, supersede the proceedings of a Committee; but such proceedings may, by Motion on Notice, be revived by Order of the House.

REPORT TO BE BROUGHT UP WITHOUT QUESTION EXCEPT IN CERTAIN CASES.

175. Every Report from a Committee of the whole House, except Reports from the Committees of Supply and Ways and Means, and Reports recommending Grants of Money or the releasing or compounding of sums of money owing to the Crown, shall be brought up without any Question being put.

RESOLUTION CANNOT BE POSTPONED.

176. A Resolution proposed in a Committee of the whole House cannot be postponed, but must be withdrawn, amended, negatived, agreed to, or superseded.

COMMITTEE CANNOT ADJOURN.

177. A Committee of the whole House cannot adjourn its own sittings, or any Debate in the Committee.

RESOLUTIONS; HOW DEALT WITH.

178. Resolutions reported from a Committee of the whole House shall be read by the Clerk a First time throughout without a Question, and a Second time one by one, a Question being put upon each, that it be agreed to; and may be agreed to or disagreed to by the House, or agreed to with Amendments, or recommitted to the Committee; or the further consideration thereof may be postponed.

CHAPTER XII.—INSTRUCTIONS AND DIRECTIONS TO COMMITTEES OF THE WHOLE HOUSE.

EFFECT OF INSTRUCTION.

179. An Instruction shall empower a Committee of the whole House to consider matters not already referred to it.

NOT TO BE MOVED AS AN AMENDMENT.

180. Before the first sitting of the Committee, an Instruction shall be proposed only as a distinct Motion after the Order of the Day for the Committee has been read, and before any Question has been proposed thereupon, and not as an Amendment to the Question, "That Mr. Speaker do now leave the Chair."

WHEN MOVED AFTER FIRST SITTING.

181. When after the first sitting of a Committee it is proposed to move a distinct Instruction, it shall be done before the Order of the Day for the Committee is read.

DIRECTION TO REPORT BY A SPECIFIED DAY.

182. When a Bill or other matter is referred to a Committee of the whole House, the House may, at the same or at any future time, order that the Bill or other matter shall be reported on a specified day; and in any such case the Bill or other matter shall be reported on or before the day so appointed, with such Amendments if any as have then been made therein by the Committee.

CHAPTER XIII.—SELECT COMMITTEES.

MR. SPEAKER NOT OBLIGED TO SERVE.

183. It shall not be obligatory on Mr. Speaker to serve on a Select Committee.

NUMBER OF MEMBERS.

184. A Select Committee shall not consist of less than five nor more than nine Members, unless the House otherwise orders.

WILLINGNESS OF MEMBERS TO ATTEND TO BE ASCERTAINED.

185. A Member intending to move for the appointment of a Select Committee shall endeavour to ascertain previously whether each Member proposed to be named by him on such Committee will give his attendance thereupon.

NOTICE TO SPECIFY NAMES.

186. A Notice of Motion for the appointment of a Select Committee shall specify the names of the Members proposed for the Committee, the mover being one, unless it is proposed that the Committee be elected by ballot.

BALLOT MAY BE ORDERED.

187. A Select Committee may be ordered to be elected by ballot.

MANNER OF BALLOTING FOR COMMITTEE.

188. When a Select Committee is ordered to be elected by ballot, each Member present shall deliver at the Table a list of the Members whom he wishes to be appointed on the Committee, not exceeding the number proposed, inclusive of the Mover; and if any list contains a larger number of names, it shall be rejected: and Mr. Speaker shall appoint two Members to be scrutineers, who, with the Clerk, shall ascertain the number of Votes for each Member; and the Members who are reported to have the greatest number of Votes shall be declared by Mr. Speaker to be the Members of the Committee; and in case two or more Members have an equality of Votes, Mr. Speaker shall decide which shall serve on the Committee.

LIST OF MEMBERS SERVING.

189. Lists of the Members serving on Select Committees shall be affixed in some conspicuous place in the lobby of the House.

MEMBER DISCHARGED AND ANOTHER APPOINTED.

190. A Member may be discharged from service on a Select Committee, and another Member appointed.

QUORUM OF SELECT COMMITTEE.

191. The quorum of a Select Committee shall be not less than half of the whole number of the Members thereof.

ELECTION OF CHAIRMAN.

192. Every Select Committee, before proceeding to any other Business, shall elect its own Chairman. In his absence the Members present shall elect a Member to act as Chairman *pro tempore.*

IF QUORUM OF MEMBERS WANTING, CHAIRMAN MAY ADJOURN.

193. If a quorum of Members is not present within half-an-hour after the time fixed for the meeting of a Select Committee, the Chairman may adjourn the meeting of the Committee to a future day.

QUORUM.

194. If at any time during the sitting of a Committee a quorum is not present, the Clerk of the Committee shall call the attention of the Chairman to the fact, who shall thereupon suspend the proceedings of the Committee until a quorum is present, or shall adjourn the Committee to a future day.

VOTE OF CHAIRMAN.

195. The Chairman of a Select Committee, not being a Select Committee on a Private Bill, shall vote in the first instance, but shall not have a casting Vote.

POWER TO SEND FOR PERSONS, PAPERS, AND RECORDS.

196. The House may give a Committee power to send for persons, papers, and records.

DAYS OF MEETINGS.

197. Select Committees may meet for the despatch of Business on any day, except Sunday, on which the House is appointed to sit, and also during any Adjournment of the House which does not exceed seven days, and, if so authorised by the House, during any longer Adjournment of the House.

NOT TO SIT WHILE HOUSE SITTING.

198. Except by leave of the House, a Select Committee shall not sit during the sitting of the House.

SELECT COMMITTEES MAY ADJOURN.

199. A Select Committee may adjourn from time to time, and, by leave of the House, from place to place.

NAMES OF MEMBERS PRESENT TO BE REPORTED.

200. The names of the Members present each day at the sitting of a Select Committee shall be entered on the Minutes of the proceedings of the Committee, and reported to the House with the Report of the Committee.

DIVISIONS TO BE REPORTED.

201. In the event of a Division taking place in a Select Committee, the Question proposed, the name of the proposer, and the Vote of each Member present, shall be entered on the Minutes of the Proceedings of the Committee, and reported to the House with the Report of the Committee.

ADMISSION AND EXCLUSION OF STRANGERS.

202. When a Committee is examining witnesses, strangers may be admitted or excluded at pleasure; but shall always be excluded when the Committee is deliberating.

COMMITTEES OPEN TO ALL MEMBERS OF HOUSE.

203. Any Member of the House shall be at liberty to be present at any meeting of a Select Committee, except while the Committee are deliberating, but shall not be allowed to speak or in any way interfere in the proceedings of the Committee unless he is a Member thereof.

CHAIRMAN TO PREPARE REPORT.

204. It shall be the duty of the Chairman of a Select Committee to prepare the Report.

PROCEEDINGS ON CONSIDERATION OF DRAFT REPORT.

205. The Chairman shall read to the Committee convened for the purpose of considering the Report, the whole of his draft Report, which shall be printed and circulated amongst the Members of the Committee; and at some subsequent meeting of the Committee the Chairman shall read the draft Report paragraph by paragraph, putting the Question to the Committee at the end of each paragraph, that it do stand part of the Report. A Member objecting to any portion of the Report shall propose his Amendment when the paragraph which he wishes to amend is under consideration. A Member disagreeing with a Report may require a statement of the reasons of his disagreement to be appended to the Report.

REPORT OF SELECT COMMITTEE TO BE SIGNED BY CHAIRMAN.

206. The Report of a Select Committee shall be signed by the Chairman on behalf of the Committee; and having been brought up by the Chairman, or by some other Member of the Committee, shall be laid upon the Table, and may be ordered to be printed or otherwise dealt with as the House may direct.

PROGRESS REPORTS.

207. A Select Committee may report, from time to time, its opinion and observations, its proceedings, or the Minutes of Evidence taken, and may also make a special Report of any matters which it may think fit to bring to the notice of the House, provided that such matters are comprised within the Order of reference.

EVIDENCE, ETC., NOT TO BE PUBLISHED.

208. The Evidence taken by a Select Committee, and Documents presented to such Committee, which have not been reported to the House, shall not be published or referred to in the House.

INSTRUCTION TO SELECT COMMITTEE.

209. An Instruction to a Select Committee may extend or restrict the Order of reference.

CHAPTER XIV.—WITNESSES.

WITNESSES NOT ATTENDING.

210. When a witness, having been duly summoned as provided by sections 41 and 42 of the "Constitution Act of 1867," does not attend pursuant to the order of the House or a Committee, his absence shall be reported and the House may order him to attend; but such order may be discharged in case the witness duly attends.

ATTENDANCE OF MEMBERS TO BE EXAMINED IN THE HOUSE.

211. When the attendance of a Member is desired, to be examined by the House or a Committee of the whole House, he shall be ordered to attend in his place.

MEMBER AS WITNESS BEFORE SELECT COMMITTEE.

212. If a Committee desires the attendance of a Member as a witness, the Chairman shall in writing request him to attend.

IF A MEMBER REFUSE TO ATTEND, ETC.

213. If a Member of the House refuses or neglects, upon being requested, to come or to give evidence or information as a witness to a Committee, the Committee shall report the refusal or neglect to the House.

COMMITTEE TO ACQUAINT HOUSE OF CHARGES AGAINST MEMBER.

214. If information comes before a Committee that charges a Member of the House, the Committee shall report the matter of such information to the House, without proceeding further thereupon.

MESSAGE FOR ATTENDANCE OF MEMBER OR OFFICER OF THE LEGISLATIVE COUNCIL.

215. When the attendance of a Member of the Legislative Council or of an officer of that House is desired, in order that he may be examined by the House, or by a Committee (not being a Committee on a Private Bill), a Message shall be sent to the Council to request that the Council give leave to such Member or officer to attend, in order to his being examined upon the matters stated in the Message.

WITNESSES NOT EXAMINED ON OATH EXCEPT IN CERTAIN CASES.

16. *Witnesses are not examined upon oath by the House, or a Committee, except in cases provided for by Statute.*

WITNESS EXAMINED BY MR. SPEAKER.

216. When a witness appears before the House, Mr. Speaker shall examine the witness, and no other Member shall put any Question otherwise than through Mr. Speaker, except by leave of the House.

WITNESS TO WITHDRAW DURING DISCUSSION.

217. If a Question is objected to, or other matter of Debate arises, the witness shall withdraw while the same is under discussion.

A MEMBER SHALL BE EXAMINED IN HIS PLACE.

218. A Member of the House shall be examined in his place.

ANY MEMBER MAY PUT QUESTIONS IN COMMITTEE.

219. In a Committee of the whole House any Member may put Questions to a witness.

CHAPTER XV.—MESSAGES.

MESSENGER INTRODUCED.

220. When a Message from the Governor is announced, the Business before the House shall be suspended, and the bearer of the Message shall be introduced.

MESSAGE TO BE READ AND CONSIDERED.

221. Mr. Speaker shall immediately read the Message to the House, and, if necessary, the House shall fix a future day for taking, or shall forthwith take, the Message into consideration.

MESSAGE FROM COUNCIL; HOW RECEIVED.

222. The bearer of a Message from the Council, not being an officer of that House, shall be introduced by the Sergeant, and conducted to the Table, where he shall deliver the Message.

MESSAGES TO COUNCIL; HOW COMMUNICATED.

223. Messages to the Council shall be in writing and shall be communicated by the Clerk-Assistant of the House, unless the House otherwise directs.

CHAPTER XVI.—PETITIONS.

ORDER OF PRESENTING PETITIONS.

224. A Petition may be presented on any day when the House is sitting, but shall not be presented during a Debate, nor after the House has proceeded to the Notices of Motion or Orders of the Day; except in the case of Petitions referring to the Question before the House, which may be received immediately upon Mr. Speaker calling the Member who has given the Notice of Motion, or upon the reading of the Order of the Day.

PETITIONS MAY BE WRITTEN OR PRINTED.

225. A Petition shall be fairly written or printed, and shall be free from erasures and interlineations.

TO CONTAIN A PRAYER AT THE END.

226. A Petition must contain a prayer at the end thereof.

TO BE SIGNED ON THE SAME SKIN OR SHEET.

227. A Petition must be signed by at least one person on the skin or sheet on which the Petition is written or printed.

TO BE IN ENGLISH OR WITH A CERTIFIED TRANSLATION.

228. A Petition shall be in the English language, or shall be accompanied by a translation, certified by the Member who presents it to be true and correct.

TO BE SIGNED BY THE PARTIES.

229. A Petition shall be signed by the persons whose names are appended to it, by their names or marks, and by no one else, except in case of incapacity from sickness.

SIGNATURES NOT TO BE TRANSFERRED.

230. The signatures shall be written upon the Petition itself, and not pasted upon it, or otherwise transferred to it.

PETITIONS OF CORPORATIONS.

231. Petitions of Corporations aggregate must be under their common seal.

NO LETTERS OR AFFIDAVITS TO BE ATTACHED.

232. Letters, affidavits, or other documents may not be attached to a Petition.

NO APPLICATION FOR PUBLIC MONEY UNLESS RECOMMENDED BY THE CROWN.

233. Application shall not be made by a Petition for any grant of public money, nor for compounding debts due to the Crown, nor for the remission of duties payable by any person, unless it be recommended by the Governor.

MEMBER PRESENTING PETITION PREVIOUSLY TO PERUSE SAME.

234. A Member presenting a Petition must acquaint himself with the contents of it, and ascertain that it does not contain language disrespectful to the House.

MEMBER TO AFFIX HIS NAME.

235. A Member presenting a Petition shall affix his name at the beginning thereof.

MEMBERS TO TAKE CARE THAT PETITION IS IN CONFORMITY WITH THE RULES.

236. A Member presenting a Petition shall take care that it is in conformity with the Standing Rules and Orders.

PETITIONS TO BE RESPECTFUL.

237. A Petition must be respectful, decorous, and temperate in its language.

PETITIONS MUST BE PRESENTED BY MEMBERS.

238. A Petition can only be presented to the House by a Member.

PETITIONS FROM MEMBERS.

239. A Member cannot present a Petition from himself.

MEMBERS CONFINED TO STATEMENTS OF CERTAIN FACTS.

240. A Member offering to present a Petition to the House shall confine himself to a statement of the persons from whom it comes, the number of signatures attached to it, and the material allegations contained in it, and to the reading of the prayer of the Petition.

C

NOT TO BE DEBATED, BUT MAY BE READ BY THE CLERK.

241. A Petition not containing matter in breach of the privileges of this House, and which according to the Standing Rules and Orders can be received, shall be brought to the Table by direction of Mr. Speaker, who shall not allow any Member to speak upon, or in relation to, such Petition; but it may be read by the Clerk at the Table, if ordered by the House.

PETITIONS MAY BE ORDERED TO BE RECEIVED.

242. A Petition having been presented (and read, if so ordered by the House), a Question shall be put, "That the Petition be received."

PETITIONS COMPLAINING OF GRIEVANCES.

243. If a Petition complains of some present personal grievance, for which there may be an urgent necessity to provide an immediate remedy, the matter contained in the Petition may be brought into discussion immediately on the presentation.

CHAPTER XVII.—PUBLIC BILLS.

BILLS ORDERED.

244. A Bill originating in this House shall be brought in upon Motion made and Question put, "That leave be given to bring in the Bill," unless it has been directed to be brought in by Resolution of the House.

BILLS ON SPECIAL SUBJECTS.

245. Bills relating to finance or trade, or imposing taxes, or authorising the expenditure of money, shall be brought in upon a Resolution reported from a Committee of the whole House and adopted by the House.

FORM OF STATEMENT OF ENACTING AUTHORITY.

17. *The following form is used in Bills as the statement of the enacting authority:—"Be it enacted by the Queen's Most Excellent Majesty, by and with the advice and consent of the Legislative Council and Legislative Assembly of Queensland in Parliament assembled, and by the authority of the same, as follows."*

BILLS PRESENTED BY A MEMBER.

246. A Bill shall be presented by the Member who has obtained leave to bring in the same, and immediately after the presentation of the Bill the Question shall be put, "That the Bill be now read a First time."

FIRST READING AND PRINTING WITHOUT DEBATE.

247. When a Bill is presented, the Questions, "That the Bill be now read a First time," and "That the Bill be printed," shall be put without Amendment or Debate.

BILLS BROUGHT FROM LEGISLATIVE COUNCIL.

248. When a Bill is brought from the Legislative Council the like Questions shall be put without Amendment or Debate.

BILL ORDERED TO BE READ A SECOND TIME.

249. When a Bill has been read the First time, it shall be ordered to be read a Second time on a future day.

QUESTION FOR SECOND READING.

250. The Order of the Day for the Second reading of a Bill being read, and a Motion being made, the Question shall be put, "That the Bill be now read a Second time."

AMENDMENTS.

251. Amendments may be proposed to such Question, by omitting the word "now," and at the end of the Question adding "on this day Three months," "on this day Six months," or any other time; or that the Bill be withdrawn or rejected.

AMENDMENTS TO BE RELEVANT.

252. Any other Amendment may be proposed to such Question provided that the Amendment is strictly relevant to the Bill.

ANOTHER BILL MAY BE BROUGHT IN ON SAME ORDER.

253. The Order for the Second reading or any future stage of a Bill having been read, may be discharged, and the House may order the Bill to be withdrawn, and may thereupon direct the Order for the introduction of the Bill to be read, and may give leave to bring in another Bill upon that Order.

COMMITTED.

254. A Bill, having been read the Second time, shall be ordered to be committed to a Committee of the whole House, either then or at a future time, or it may first be referred to a Select Committee.

PREAMBLE TO BE POSTPONED.

255. When a Bill has been committed to a Committee of the whole House, the Preamble, if any, shall be postponed until after the Clauses and Schedules of the Bill have been considered.

QUESTION ON EACH CLAUSE.

256. The Chairman shall put a Question on each Clause of the Bill, "That the Clause, as read, stand part of the Bill."

AMENDMENTS TO CLAUSES.

257. Such Question being proposed, Amendments may be proposed to the Clause—
  (1) To omit words;
  (2) To omit words in order to add or insert other words instead thereof;
  (3) To add or insert words.

And such Amendments shall be dealt with as in the House itself.

DEBATE TO BE RELEVANT.

258. When a Clause or Amendment is under discussion, a Member speaking shall confine himself to the matter of that Clause or Amendment.

QUESTION ON CLAUSE, AS AMENDED.

259. When a Clause has been amended, a Question shall be put "That the Clause, as amended, stand part of the Bill."

WHAT AMENDMENTS ADMISSIBLE: TITLE AMENDED.

260. Any Amendment may be made to a Clause or other part of a Bill, provided that the Amendment is relevant to the subject matter of the Bill, or pursuant to an Instruction, and is otherwise in conformity with the Standing Rules and Orders of the House; but, if an Amendment is agreed to which is not within the Title of the Bill, the Committee shall amend the Title accordingly, and report the Amendment specially to the House.

CLAUSES POSTPONED.

261. A Clause may be postponed whether it has been amended or not.

NEW CLAUSES OR SCHEDULES.

262. When it is proposed to add a Clause or Schedule in Committee, such Clause or Schedule shall be proposed when the Committee has arrived at the part of the Bill at which it is proposed to be inserted.

TO BE READ.

263. A Clause or Schedule, proposed to be added in Committee, shall be read a First time without any Question put, and a Second time on Motion made and Question put.

CLAUSES MADE PART OF BILL.

264. A Clause or Schedule, proposed to be added in Committee, having been read the First and Second time, the Question shall be put by the Chairman, "That the Clause (or Schedule) do stand part of the Bill"; and the Clause or Schedule may thereupon be amended or otherwise dealt with as in other cases.

PREAMBLE.

265. After all the Clauses and Schedules have been gone through, and new Clauses or Schedules (if any) added, the Preamble (if any) shall be considered, and, if necessary, amended; and a Question shall be put, "That this be the Preamble of the Bill."

REPORT OF BILL.

266. The Bill having been fully considered, the Chairman shall be directed to report the Bill without Amendment, or to report the Bill with the Amendments.

BILL REPORTED WITHOUT AMENDMENT.

267. A Bill, being reported without Amendment, shall be ordered to be read a Third time on a future day.

BILL REPORTED WITH AMENDMENTS.

268. When Amendments have been made to a Bill, the Report shall be received without Debate, and the Bill, as amended, shall be ordered to be taken into consideration then, or on a future day.

AMENDMENTS, HOW DEALT WITH.

269. When the amended Bill is under consideration, the Amendments made in Committee shall be read by the Clerk a First time throughout, and a Second time, on Motion, one by one, a Question being put upon each, "That the Amendment be agreed to"; which Amendment may be agreed to, disagreed to, or amended.

ON CONSIDERATION, FURTHER AMENDMENTS MAY BE MADE.

270. On consideration of the Bill as amended, further Amendments may be made to any part thereof, and new Clauses or Schedules added; but no Clause or Schedule shall be offered on consideration of the Bill as amended, without Notice: or the Bill may be recommitted.

NEW CLAUSES AT REPORT STAGE.

271. A Clause or Schedule proposed to be added on consideration of the Bill as amended shall be read a First and Second time in the same manner as in Committee, after which the Question shall be put, "That the Clause (or Schedule) do stand part of the Bill," and the Clause or Schedule may thereupon be amended or otherwise dealt with as in other cases.

AMENDMENTS ON RECOMMITTAL—CONSIDERATION.

272. When Amendments have been made to a Bill on recommittal, the Bill as amended shall be taken into consideration at once or on a future day in the same manner as upon the first Report.

THIRD READING.

273. When all Amendments have been agreed to or otherwise disposed of, the Bill shall be ordered to be read a Third time on a future day.

AMENDMENTS OR RECOMMITTAL ON THIRD READING.

274. Verbal Amendments, but no other, may be made to a Bill on the Third reading; but the Order of the Day for the Third reading may be discharged, and the Bill, in respect to the whole or any part, may be recommitted, when any Amendments, of which Notice has been given, may be made.

QUESTION FOR THIRD READING.

275. The Order of the Day for the Third reading of a Bill being read, and a Motion being made, a Question shall be put, "That the Bill be now read a Third time," to which Question Amendments may be moved, as on the Second reading.

PASSING AND TITLE.

276. After the Third reading, a Question shall be put, "That the Bill do pass"; after which the Title of the Bill shall be read by Mr. Speaker, and a Question put, "That this be the Title of the Bill," which may be agreed to, or agreed to with Amendments.

PROCEEDINGS ON THIRD READING ADJOURNED.

277. The further proceedings consequent on the Third reading may be adjourned to a future day.

CLERK TO CERTIFY PASSING OF BILL.

278. When a Bill is passed by the House, the Clerk shall certify at the top of the first page the date of its Passing.

BILLS PASSED WITH UNUSUAL EXPEDITION.

279. Bills of an urgent nature may, by leave of the House, be passed with unusual expedition through their several stages.

TEMPORARY LAWS.

280. The precise duration of every temporary law shall be expressed in a distinct clause at the end of the Bill.

BILLS SENT TO LEGISLATIVE COUNCIL.

281. When all the proceedings on a Bill have been concluded, the Bill shall be ordered to be carried to the Legislative Council with a Message to desire their concurrence ; or if the Bill was brought from the Legislative Council, "to acquaint the Legislative Council that this House has agreed to the same without Amendment," or "with Amendments in which this House desires the concurrence of the Legislative Council."

BILLS RETURNED FROM LEGISLATIVE COUNCIL WITH AMENDMENTS.

282. When a Bill is returned from the Legislative Council with Amendments, such Amendments shall be considered in Committee of the whole House and agreed to, or agreed to with Amendments, or disagreed to, or the further consideration thereof may be put off for Three or Six months, or the Bill may be ordered to be laid aside.

AMENDMENTS BY THE COUNCIL TO BE CONSIDERED.

283. Amendments by the Council to Bills shall be appointed to be considered on a future day, unless the House orders them to be considered forthwith.

AMENDMENTS PROPOSED BY THE GOVERNOR.

284. When the Governor transmits by Message to this House any Amendment which he desires to be made in a Bill presented to him for Her Majesty's assent, the Amendment shall be dealt with in the same manner as Amendments proposed by the Legislative Council.

WHEN GOVERNOR'S AMENDMENTS ARE AGREED TO, TO BE SENT TO LEGISLATIVE COUNCIL.

285. When this House has agreed to an Amendment proposed by the Governor, such Amendment shall be forwarded to the Legislative Council with a Message to desire their concurrence.

BILLS REQUIRING UNUSUAL MAJORITY; HOW CERTIFIED.

286. When a Bill which requires an unusual majority has been read the Second time and the Third time in this House with the prescribed majority, The Clerk shall certify accordingly.

CHAPTER XVIII.—PRIVATE BILLS.

NOTICE TO APPLY FOR PRIVATE BILL TO BE PUBLISHED IN "GAZETTE."

287. Notice of the intention to apply for leave to bring in a Private Bill shall be published once a week, for four consecutive weeks, in the *Gazette*, in one or more public newspapers published in Brisbane, and in one or more public newspapers published in or nearest to the district affected by the Bill, which notice shall contain a true statement of the general objects of the Bill.

INITIATION OF PRIVATE BILL.

288. A Private Bill shall not be initiated in this House but upon a Petition first presented and received, with a printed copy of the proposed Bill annexed; and such Petition shall be signed by one or more of the persons applying for leave to introduce the Bill.

PETITION FOR PRIVATE BILL TO SET FORTH THAT DUE NOTICE HAS BEEN PUBLISHED, ETC., ETC.

289. A Petition for a Private Bill shall commence by setting forth that within the three months previous to its presentation to this House, the public notice required by the Standing Rules and Orders has been duly given, setting forth the general objects of the Bill and the intention to apply for leave to bring it in, and shall conclude with a true statement of the general objects of the Bill, and a prayer for leave to bring it in; and the production of the numbers of the *Gazette* and newspaper or newspapers containing the notice shall be sufficient proof of the notice.

WHEN PETITION HAS BEEN RECEIVED.

290. When the Petition has been received, Notice of Motion for leave to bring in the Bill may be given, and the Bill must be brought in within thirty days from the presentation of the Petition.

WHEN LEAVE TO BRING IN HAS BEEN GIVEN.

291. When leave to bring in a Private Bill has been given, and before the Bill is read a First time, it shall be printed at the expense of the persons applying for leave to bring it in, in the same form as that commonly used in respect of Public Bills, and a sufficient number of printed copies of the Bill shall be delivered to the Clerk, for the use of the House.

DEPOSIT.

292. Before a Private Bill is read a First time, the sum of twenty-five pounds, to meet the expenses attendant on the Bill, shall be paid to the credit of the Consolidated Revenue Fund, and a certificate of such payment shall be produced by the Member having charge of the Bill.

TO BE REFERRED TO SELECT COMMITTEE.

293. When a Private Bill has been read the First time, it shall be referred to a Select Committee, to be appointed on Motion upon Notice, and such Committee shall require proof of the allegations contained in the Preamble.

CHAIRMAN'S VOTE.

294. The Chairman of the Committee shall have a vote in the first instance, and also a casting vote.

PRIVATE BILLS COMING FROM THE LEGISLATIVE COUNCIL.

295. A Private Bill brought to this House from the Legislative Council, if accompanied by printed copies of the Report and proceedings of the Select Committee to which it has been referred by the Legislative Council, shall be proceeded with in all respects in the same manner as Public Bills first presented in this House, unless the House otherwise orders.

OPPOSING PETITIONS.

296. A Petition in opposition to a Private Bill shall distinctly specify the grounds of such opposition ; and, if received, shall be referred to the Select Committee, if any, on the Bill.

A SELECT COMMITTEE MAY HEAR COUNSEL, ETC.

297. A Select Committee on a Private Bill may, in its discretion, hear counsel if it is desired ; and may also take such oral or other evidence as it may think requisite ; and may decide on matters in issue between the persons promoting and opposing the Bill ; after which, the Question shall be put from the Chair, "That this Preamble stand part of the Bill," whereupon the Preamble may be amended : And if it is amended the Question shall be put, "That this Preamble as amended stand part of the Bill": And if the Question "That this Preamble" or "That this Preamble as amended" stand part of the Bill pass in the Negative, the Bill shall be rejected, and the Committee shall report accordingly ; but if the Question pass in the Affirmative, the several clauses of the Bill shall next be proceeded with, and the Amendments, if any, noted for report to the House, care being taken that no clause be inserted or Amendment made in the Bill which is foreign to the import of the notice required under these Standing Rules and Orders to be given by the persons applying for leave to bring it in.

WHEN SELECT COMMITTEE HAS REPORTED IN FAVOUR.

298. When a Select Committee has reported in favour of a Private Bill, the Bill shall be ordered to be read a Second time on a future day, and shall be proceeded with as in the case of Public Bills. Printed copies of the Report and evidence shall be furnished to Members before the day so appointed.

CHAPTER XIX.—ACCOUNTS, PAPERS, AND PRINTING.

ACCOUNTS, ETC., ORDERED.

299. Accounts and papers may be ordered to be laid upon the Table of the House.

ADDRESS FOR PAPERS.

300. When the Royal prerogative is concerned in any account or paper, an Address shall be presented to the Governor praying that the same may be laid upon the Table of the House.

PAPERS PRESENTED BY STATUTE OR BY COMMAND.

301. Other papers may be presented pursuant to Statute or by command of the Governor.

DOCUMENTS READ OR CITED BY MEMBER.

302. A document read or cited by a Member may be ordered to be laid upon the Table.

UNFURNISHED RETURNS.

303. On every Wednesday, when the House is sitting, the Clerk shall read out the titles of all Orders and Addresses for Returns previously agreed to by the House and not furnished.

APPOINTMENT OF PRINTING COMMITTEE.

304. At the commencement of each Session a Select Committee shall be appointed to assist Mr. Speaker in all matters which relate to the printing to be executed by order of the House, and for the purpose of selecting and arranging for printing Petitions, Returns, and other papers.

ORDERED TO BE PRINTED.

305. Accounts and papers may be ordered to be printed.

CHAPTER XX.—SUPPLY, AND WAYS AND MEANS.

PENALTIES, FORFEITURE, AND FEES.

306. When a Bill is brought to the House from the Legislative Council, or is returned by the Legislative Council to the House with Amendments, whereby a pecuniary penalty, forfeiture, or fee is authorised, imposed, appropriated, regulated, varied, or extinguished, the House will not insist on its Privileges in the following cases :—

(1) When the object of such pecuniary penalty or forfeiture is to secure the execution of the Bill, or the punishment or prevention of offences ;

(2) When the fees are imposed in respect of benefits taken or services rendered under the Bill, and in order to the execution of the Bill, and are not made payable into the Treasury, or in aid of the Public Revenue, and do not form the ground of public accounting by the parties receiving the same, either in respect of deficit or surplus ;

(3) When the Bill is a Private Bill.

OPENING OF COMMITTEE OF SUPPLY.

307. The Order of the Day being read for the House to resolve itself into the Committee of Supply, the Governor's Speech to both Houses of Parliament shall be ordered to be referred to the Committee, together with any Estimates that may have been transmitted by Message.

PETITION, MOTION, OR BILL, FOR GRANTING MONEY.

308. The House will not proceed upon any Petition, Motion, or Bill, for granting any money or for releasing or compounding any sum of money owing to the Crown, except in a Committee of the whole House.

MOTION FOR ANY PUBLIC AID OR CHARGE UPON THE PEOPLE.

309. If a Motion is made in the House for any public aid or charge upon the people, the consideration and Debate thereof may not be presently entered upon, but shall be referred to a Committee of the whole House, which shall be appointed to sit on a future day.

MOTION FOR ADDRESS TO THE CROWN PRAYING THAT MONEY MAY BE ISSUED.

310. The House will not proceed upon a Motion for an Address to the Crown, praying that any money may be issued, or that any expense may be incurred, except in Committee of the whole House.

MOTION IN COMMITTEE OF SUPPLY TO OMIT OR REDUCE ANY ITEM.

311. When a Motion is made in Committee of Supply to omit or reduce any item of a vote, a Question shall be proposed from the Chair for omitting or reducing such item accordingly ; and Members shall speak to that Question only, until it has been disposed of.

ORDER IN WHICH MOTIONS ARE TO BE TAKEN.

312. When several Motions are offered, they shall be taken in the order in which the items to which they relate appear in the printed Estimates.

AFTER A QUESTION FOR OMITTING AN ITEM HAS BEEN DISPOSED OF.

313. After a Question for omitting or reducing an item has been disposed of, a Motion shall not be made nor Debate allowed upon any preceding item.

PROPOSITION TO OMIT OR REDUCE ITEMS.

314. When it has been proposed to omit an item in a vote, the Question shall be afterwards put upon the original vote, or upon the reduced vote, as the case may be, without further Amendment except as to subsequent items.

WHEN REDUCTION IS PROPOSED.

315. When a reduction of the amount of an item or vote is proposed, the Question shall be first put upon the smaller sum ; and, if that is negatived, then upon the next larger sum ; and so on, until the Question is put upon the original vote, after failure of the several Motions for a reduction thereof.

ESTIMATE OR ITEM MAY BE POSTPONED.

316. At any time during the discussion of an Estimate, or item in an Estimate, such Estimate or item may be ordered to be postponed, whether it has been amended or not, either until the whole of the Estimates or Supplementary Estimates for the year for which the proposed vote is intended to be taken, or some specified part of those Estimates, has been disposed of.

COMMITTEE OF WAYS AND MEANS APPOINTED.

317. When the first Resolution of the Committee of Supply has been agreed to, a Question shall be put, "That this House will on a future day resolve itself into a Committee to consider of Ways and Means for raising the Supply granted to Her Majesty," which Committee is the Committee of Ways and Means.

RESOLUTIONS TO BE RECEIVED ON A FUTURE DAY.

318. When a Resolution is reported from the Committee of Supply or Committee of Ways and Means, or a Resolution is reported from a Committee of the Whole House, recommending a grant of money or the releasing or compounding of a sum of money owing to the Crown, the Resolution shall be ordered to be received on a future day.

MANNER IN WHICH RESOLUTIONS ARE DEALT WITH.

319. Resolutions of the Committees of Supply and Ways and Means reported to the House may be agreed to, amended, re-committed, or disagreed to ; or their consideration may be postponed.

CHARGE ON PEOPLE NOT TO BE INCREASED.

320. An Amendment, whereby the charge upon the people will be increased, may not be made to any such Resolution, unless the charge so increased will not exceed the charge already existing by virtue of some Act of Parliament.

CHAPTER XXI.—CONTEMPT.

PERSON CHARGED WITH CONTEMPT TO BE SUMMONED.

321. When it is made to appear to the House that any person has committed any of the offences enumerated in the forty-fifth section of the "*Constitution Act of* 1867," a Motion shall be made, and Question put, that such person be ordered to attend at the Bar of the House, on a day and at an hour to be named, and if the Question passes in the Affirmative, a copy of the order of the House, specifying the nature of the offence, in the words of the Act or in similar words, and

requiring the attendance of such person, and certified by the Clerk, shall be served upon him either personally or by prepaid post letter addressed to him at his usual or last known place of abode in Queensland.

QUARRELS NOT TO BE PROSECUTED.

18. *A Member is not permitted to prosecute a quarrel with another Member arising out of Debates or Proceedings of the House, or any Committee thereof.*

PROCEEDINGS IF THE PERSON CHARGED ATTENDS.

322. If on the day and at the hour so appointed the person so charged attends according to the exigency of the order, Mr. Speaker shall inform him of the nature of the charge, and he shall be heard in his defence, either personally or by counsel, after which the House may adjudge him to be guilty of the offence charged against him, or may direct that he be discharged.

PROCEEDINGS IF HE DOES NOT ATTEND.

323. If the person so charged does not attend, then, upon proof to the satisfaction of the House of due service of a copy of the order upon him, the House may deal with him in like manner.

PUNISHMENT OF PERSON ADJUDGED GUILTY OF CONTEMPT.

324. When the House has adjudged a person guilty of the offence charged against him, the House may adjudge him to pay a fine not exceeding five hundred pounds, and in the event of the fine not being paid immediately, or within such time as the House may allow, to be imprisoned in the custody of the Sergeant-at-Arms in such place as the House may direct, or in Her Majesty's Gaol at Brisbane, until the fine has been paid, or until the end of the existing Session, or for such shorter period as the House by the same or any subsequent order may direct.

TO BE COMMITTED TO CUSTODY OF THE SERGEANT-AT-ARMS.

225. When a person is so ordered to be imprisoned, he shall be committed to the custody of the Sergeant-at-Arms, or the keeper of Her Majesty's Gaol at Brisbane, by warrant signed by Mr. Speaker, which shall set forth in the words of the "*Constitution Act of* 1867" or in similar words, the nature of the offence of which he has been adjudged guilty.

FEES ON ARREST.

326. In addition to any fine imposed by the House by way of punishment, the following fees shall be payable to the Sergeant-at-Arms by any person apprehended by order of the House or of Mr. Speaker, and no person shall, without the express direction of the House, be discharged out of custody until such fees are paid or the Session is ended :—

Fees.

For arrest £10 0 0
For each day's detention, including sustenance 2 0 0
For conveyance to place of custody, five shillings per mile.

CHAPTER XXII.—DUTIES OF THE CLERK OF THE ASSEMBLY.

VOTES AND PROCEEDINGS—JOURNALS.

327. The Votes and Proceedings of the House and of Committees of the whole House shall be noted by the Clerk at the Table, and the Votes and Proceedings, having been first perused by Mr. Speaker, shall be printed ; and the Votes and Proceedings shall be signed by Mr. Speaker and the Clerk, and shall be the Journals of the Legislative Assembly.

RECORD OF ATTENDANCE OF MEMBERS.

328. The names of the Members present at each sitting of the House, or, if there is no quorum present at the time appointed for the meeting of the House, the names of the Members then present, shall be entered in the Journals.

COPIES OF PAPERS FOR MEMBERS.

329. Every Member shall be furnished by the Clerk with one copy of each paper printed by order of the House, as it issues complete from the Press, except in the case of the Votes and Proceedings, of which he shall be furnished with a proof copy as soon as practicable after each sitting of the House : and the Table of the House shall be supplied with as many copies of each document to which the Business Paper of the Day has reference as there are Members : which copies shall be for the use of Members within the precincts of the House only. Mr. Speaker may, however, direct the Clerk to supply an additional copy to any Member who may have lost that originally supplied to him.

CUSTODY OF RECORDS.

330. The custody of the Journals and Records, and of all documents whatsoever laid before the House, shall be in the Clerk; who shall neither take, nor permit to be taken, any of such Journals, Records, or documents from the offices of the House, without the express leave or order of the House. Provided, however, that, in the event of the House being adjourned for any period longer than seven days, or prorogued, such leave may be given by Mr. Speaker, who shall report the same to the House upon its re-assembling.

CHAPTER XXIII.—MISCELLANEOUS.

CONSEQUENCES OF SUSPENSION.

331. When a Member is suspended from the service of the House, he shall be excluded from the House and from all rooms set apart for the use of Members.

ADMISSION OF STRANGERS.

332. Mr. Speaker only shall have the privilege of admitting strangers to the Galleries of the House.

WITHDRAWAL OF STRANGERS.

333. If at any sitting of the House, or in Committee of the whole House, any Member takes notice that strangers are present, Mr. Speaker, or the Chairman, as the case may be, shall forthwith put the Question that strangers be ordered to withdraw, which Question shall be decided without Debate : But Mr. Speaker or the Chairman may, whenever he thinks fit, order the withdrawal of strangers from any part of the House.

STANDING ORDERS MAY BE SUSPENDED.

334. Any of the foregoing Standing Rules and Orders may be suspended or dispensed with by the House ; but a Motion shall not be made to suspend or dispense with any such Rules or Orders without due Notice thereof, except by leave of the House, which leave shall not be granted if six Members dissent therefrom.

HOUSE OF COMMONS RULES ADOPTED.

335. In all cases not specially provided for by these Standing Rules and Orders, or by Sessional or other Orders, resort shall be had to the Rules, Forms, and Usages of the Commons House of Parliament of Great Britain and Ireland as existing at the date of the passing of these Standing Rules and Orders, which shall be followed and observed so far as the same can apply to the proceedings of the House.

REPEAL.

336. All Standing Rules and Orders of the Legislative Assembly heretofore made are repealed and annulled.

JOINT
STANDING RULES AND ORDERS

OF THE

LEGISLATIVE COUNCIL & LEGISLATIVE ASSEMBLY.

I.—MESSAGES.

COMMUNICATIONS TO BE BY MESSAGE.

1. All communications between the Council and Assembly shall be by message.

TO BE TRANSMITTED BY CLERK-ASSISTANT, UNLESS OTHERWISE ORDERED.

2. Messages from one House to the other shall be in writing, and shall be communicated by the Clerk-Assistant of each House respectively, unless the House transmitting the message shall otherwise direct.

MEMBERS CARRYING MESSAGE, HOW ANNOUNCED.

3. Members carrying any message from either House of the Legislature to the other shall be announced at once, unless any Member shall be addressing the House, or unless the President or Speaker, as the case may be, shall be ascertaining the sense of the House upon any question, in which case the bearer of the message shall not be announced until the Member shall have concluded his speech, or until the sense of the House shall have been declared by the President or Speaker, as the case may be; and the bearer of the message shall be introduced by the Usher or Sergeant-at-Arms, and shall deliver the message to the President or Speaker.

MESSAGE CARRIED BY THE CLERK.

4. Messages carried by The Clerk of either House shall be delivered to the Usher or Sergeant-at-Arms, as the case may be.

CONSENT DESIRED TO BILLS, VOTES, AND RESOLUTIONS, HOW COMMUNICATED.

5. Bills, Votes, and Resolutions of either House of the Legislature, to which the consent of the other House shall be desired, shall be communicated to such other House by message; and, in the first instance, without any reason being assigned for the passing such Bill, Vote, or Resolution.

SAME COURSE WHEN RETURNING.

6. Bills, Votes, and Resolutions of either House of the Legislature, to which the consent of the other House shall have been desired, shall, if returned from such other House, be sent by message; and, in the first instance, without any reason being assigned for passing, declining to assent to, or amending, as the case may be, such Bills, Votes, or Resolutions.

AMENDMENTS INSISTED UPON, AND COMMUNICATIONS DESIRED; REASONS TO BE STATED IN MESSAGE.

7. When either House of the Legislature shall not agree to any amendment made by the other House in any Bill, Vote, or other Resolution with which its concurrence shall have been desired, or when either House shall insist upon any amendment previously proposed by such House, and any communication shall be desired, then the communication shall· be by message; and the House transmitting such message shall at the same time transmit written reasons for not agreeing to the amendment proposed by the other House, or for insisting upon any amendment previously proposed by the House sending such message.

JOINT COMMITTEES; LIBRARY, REFRESHMENT ROOM, PARLIAMENTARY BUILDINGS.

8. At the commencement of each Session there shall be appointed by each House a Committee of three members respectively to constitute a Joint Committee to manage the Library; another Committee of three Members of each House respectively to constitute a Joint Committee for the management of the Refreshment Rooms; another Committee of three Members of each House respectively to constitute a Joint Committee for the management and superintendence of the Parliament Buildings; and three Members shall form a quorum of each of the said Committees.

PROPOSAL FOR JOINT COMMITTEE TO STATE OBJECT AND NUMBER.— TIME AND PLACE OF MEETING.

9. Every proposal for a Joint Committee not provided for in these Rules shall be by message; shall state the object of such Committee, the number of Members to serve thereon, being not less than six, and the number of Members to form a quorum thereof; and the House whose concurrence shall be desired shall name the time and place of meeting.

II.—BILLS.

BILLS TO BE FAIR PRINTED AS CERTIFIED.

10. Every Bill shall be printed fair immediately after it shall have been passed in the House in which it originated; and The Clerk of the House in which the Bill shall have passed shall certify the passing thereof on such fair print, together with the day upon which the Bill did pass.

AMENDMENTS TO BE WRITTEN ON PAPER ATTACHED TO THE BILL, AND CERTIFIED BY THE CLERK.

11. If any amendment shall be made by the House to which the Bill shall be sent, such amendment shall be written on paper and attached to the Bill, and reference shall be made to the section and line of the Bill where the words are to be inserted or omitted, as the case may be, and such amendment shall be certified by The Clerk of the House in which it shall have passed.

GOVERNMENT PRINTER TO FURNISH THREE COPIES OF BILL, ON VELLUM, TO CLERK OF PARLIAMENTS.

12. When such Bill shall have passed both Houses of the Legislature, it shall be fair printed by the Government Printer, who shall furnish three fair prints thereof on vellum to The Clerk of the Parliaments.

FAIR PRINTS TO BE AUTHENTICATED BY HIM.

13. Such three fair prints of each Bill shall be duly authenticated by The Clerk of the Parliaments.

CLERK OF PARLIAMENTS TO PRESENT ALL BILLS, EXCEPT APPROPRIATION BILL, TO THE GOVERNOR.

14. The three fair prints of all Bills, except the Appropriation Bill, when passed, shall be presented to the Governor for Her Majesty's assent by The Clerk of the Parliaments.

DISPOSAL OF ORIGINAL BILLS.

15. When the Governor shall have assented in the name of Her Majesty to any Bill, one of the fair prints thereof, on vellum, shall be deposited by The Clerk of the Parliaments in the Registry of the Supreme Court, another shall be delivered to the Private Secretary of His Excellency the Governor, for transmission to Her Majesty's Principal Secretary of State for the Colonies, and the third shall be retained in the record office of the Parliament Houses.

TITLE OF BILL.

16. The title of every Bill shall succinctly set forth the general object thereof.

D

BILLS TO BE NUMBERED BY THE CLERK OF THE PARLIAMENTS.

17. All public Acts assented to on behalf of Her Majesty, and all public Bills reserved for the signification of Her Majesty's pleasure, shall bo numbered by The Clerk of the Parliaments immediately before the title, in the order of such assent or reservation, with the date of such assent or reservation added next after the title ; commencing a new series of numbers with each year of Her Majesty's reign.

CLERK OF THE PARLIAMENTS.

18. The Clerk of the Legislative Council shall be Clerk of the Parliaments.

CLERK-ASSISTANT TO PERFORM DUTIES IN CASE OF ABSENCE OF THE CLERK.

19. In case of unavoidable absence or illness of The Clerk of the Parliaments, the duties imposed upon him by these rules shall be performed by the Clerk-Assistant of the Legislative Council.

CLERICAL ERROR DISCOVERED IN ANY BILL.

20. Upon the discovery of any clerical error in any Bills which shall have passed both Houses of Parliament, and before the same be presented to the Governor for the Royal assent, The Clerk of the Parliaments shall report the same to the House in which the Bill originated, which House may deal with the same as with other amendments.

III.—PRACTICE OF IMPERIAL PARLIAMENT.

CASES NOT PROVIDED FOR.

21. In all cases not herein provided for having reference to the joint action of both Houses of Parliament, resort shall be had to the rules, forms, and practice of the Imperial Parliament.

INDEX.

——:o:——

The Italic Lines indicate Rules of Practice.

	NO. OF RULE.	PAG
A.		
Absence of Chairman of Committees	11	7
Absence, unavoidable, of Speaker—Chairman takes Chair	9	7
,, temporary, during Sitting	10	7
ACCOUNTS—		
May be ordered to be laid before the House ...	299	41
May be ordered to be printed	305	41
ADDRESSES—		
Motion for Address in Reply to His Excellency's Speech made and seconded	14	8
Resolution for Address agreed to, with or without Amendment	14	8
To be presented by Mr. Speaker	15	8
To Governor, how presented	17	8
Governor's answer to be reported	18	8
In what case Accounts and Papers are procured by	300	41
Motion for, to the Crown, praying that money may be issued	310	42
ADJOURNMENT OF DEBATE	121	19
Member who has spoken to main question may speak to question of adjournment	123	19
Member may speak to main question after having spoken to	124	20
Main question not to be entered upon in speaking to	125	20
Same Member not to move Adjournment of House and	127	20
When negatived, not to be proposed again immediately	127	20
ADJOURNMENT OF THE HOUSE—		
After election of Speaker	6	6
If quorum not present... ... ,...	24, 25, 27	9, 10
Before next sitting day fixed	28	10
Except in certain cases, the House only adjourned by its own resolution	31	10
Business not disposed of at	32	10
Questions superseded by motion for	73	15
Previous question may be superseded by	76	15
Amendment not to be moved on motion for ...	98	17
Member who has spoken may not move	126	20
Same Member not to move Adjournment of Debate and...	127	20
When negatived, not to be proposed again immediately	127	20
Restrictions on motion for	130, 131	20, 21
Adjournment of Select Committees	199	29
Admission of Strangers to the House	332	46
,, ,, Select Committees	202	29

	NO. OF RULE.	PAGE.

Allegiance, Oath of, Members take	3	6
Amendments to Bills. *See* Bills.		
AMENDMENTS—		
Not to be withdrawn in absence of proposer ...	• 51	12
Must be withdrawn or negatived before original motion withdrawn	52	13
Not allowed on formal business	61	13
If irregular, Mr. Speaker shall not put the question	67	14
Same, not to be again proposed which during same Session resolved in affirmative or negative ...	71	14
Previous question precludes	74	15
Previous question shall not be moved upon ...	77	15
Forms of	83	16
If not seconded will not be entertained	84	16
Amendment to omit words	85	16
To omit words and insert or add others	86	16
To insert or add words	87	16
To former part of a question may not be proposed after a later part has been amended or proposed to be amended	88	16
Not to be made to words already agreed to ...	89	16
May by leave be withdrawn	90	16
When proposed, but not made, the question put as originally proposed	91	16
When made, main question as amended is put ...	92	16
Order in which put	93	17
When moved, original motion cannot be varied ...	94	17
Amendments to proposed amendments	95	17
Dealt with as if main question	96	17
To Order of the Day must be relevant	97	17
Not allowed on motion for adjournment	98	17
Member who has spoken may not move	126	20
No amendment entertained on going into Committee of Supply of Ways and Means	132	21
May be moved to question for Mr. Speaker to leave the Chair	155	24
To motion for second reading of Bill	251	35
Must be relevant	252	35
What amendments admissible to Bills	260	36
Amendments to Bills, how dealt with ...	269, 270, 271, 272, 274	37
Amendments to Bills by Legislative Council	282, 283	38
„ „ by Governor	284	38
APPLICATIONS FOR PUBLIC MONEY—		
To be referred to Committee of the whole House	308, 309, 310	42
Appointment of Chairman of Committees	8	7
Approbation, Royal, of Speaker elect	7, 8, 9	6, 7
Arrest, fees payable on, of person guilty of contempt ...	326	44
Assent, Royal, to Bills—J.S.O.	14	49
Attendance of Members entered in Votes and Proceedings	328	45

INDEX.

INDEX. iii.

INDEX. iii.

	NO. OF RULE.	PAGE.
B.		
Ballot for Select Committee	187, 188	28
Bar of the House, person charged with contempt to be summoned to	321	43
Bell to be rung before counting House	30	10
„ „ Committee	167	25
„ „ on Division being demanded	137	22
Benches on either side of the Chair, use of	12	9
BILLS —		
Form of statement of enacting authority	17	. 34
Amendments to stages of	89	34
How brought in	244, 245	34
On special subjects	245	34
Presented by a Member	246	34
First reading and printing	246, 247	34
Brought from Legislative Council	248	35
Ordered to be read a second time	249	35
Question for second reading	250	35
Amendments to question for second reading	251	35
Amendments to be strictly relevant	252	35
Another may be brought in on same order	253	35
Committed	254	35
Preamble to be postponed	255	35
Question on each clause	256	35
Amendments to clauses	257	35
Debate to be relevant	258	36
Question on clause as amended	259	36
What amendments admissible: title amended	260	36
Clauses postponed	261	36
New clauses or schedules	262	36
„ „ to be read	263	36
„ „ made part of Bill	264	36
Preamble	265	36
Report of	266	36
Reported, without amendment	267	37
„ with amendments	268	37
Amendments, how dealt with	269	37
On consideration, further amendments may be made	270	37
New clauses at report stage	271	37
Amendments or recommittal—consideration	272	37
Third reading ordered	273	37
Amendments or recommittal on third reading	274	37
Question for third reading	275	. 37
Passing, and title	276	38
Proceedings on third reading adjourned	277	38
Clerk to certify passing of Bill	278	38
Passed with unusual expedition	279	38
Temporary laws, duration of, to be expressed	280	38
Sent to Legislative Council with a message	281	38
Returned from Legislative Council with amendments	282	38
Amendments by the Council to be considered	283	38
Amendments proposed by Governor	284	38

	NO. OF RULE.	PAGE.
BILLS—*continued.*		
When Governor's amendments are agreed to, to be sent to Legislative Council	285	39
For altering Constitution Act, how certified ...	286	39
From the Legislative Council, relating to penalties, forfeitures, and fees	306	41
Messages respecting Bills—J.S.O.	5 to 7	48
After Bill has passed, The Clerk shall certify— J.S.O. *See also* S.O. of Assembly 278 ...	10	49
Bills to be fair printed as certified—J.S.O.... ...	10	49
Amendments in Bills—J.S.O.	11	49
After Bill has passed both Houses it is to be printed on vellum—J.S O.	12	49
And authenticated by The Clerk of the Parliaments —J.S.O.	13	49
And, excepting Appropriation Bills, to be presented by The Clerk of the Parliaments for the Royal Assent—J.S.O.	14	49
Custody of original Bills—J.S.O.	15	49
Title of Bill—J.S.O.	16	49
Numbering Bills—J.S.O.	17	50
Correction of errors in Bills—J.S.O.	20	50
See also Private Bills.		
Buildings, Parliamentary—J.S.O.	8	48
BUSINESS—		
House appoints days for despatch of	23	9
Not disposed of at adjournment	32	10
Under discussion on adjournment (no quorum) ...	32	
„ „ adjourned under S.O. giving precedence to other business ...	32	
Superseded in certain cases, lapses	32	
Private notices and orders alternate...	33	
Order on Government days	58	13
Formal or unopposed	59	13
Not prevented by the disposal of formal motions or orders	62	14
Notices relating to business of House take precedence	62	13
See also Bills, Notices of Motion, Orders of the Day.		

C.

Cases not provided for by Standing Orders	335	46
„ „ „ —J.S.O. ...	21	50
CASTING VOTES—		
When votes are equal (on a division) Mr. Speaker gives a casting vote	147	23
Any reasons stated by him to be entered in the Votes and Proceedings	147	23
In Committee of the Whole House, Chairman gives a casting voice	158	24
Of Chairman of Select Committee on Private Bill...	294	40

—	NO. OF RULE.	PAGE.
CHAIR—		
Member, if elected Speaker without opposition, called to the, without question put	5	6
Member moving about the House to make obeisance to the	20	9
Member may not pass between Chair and Member speaking, nor between Chair and Table	21	9
Mr. Speaker to take the, as soon after the hour appointed for meeting of the Assembly as there shall be a quorum present	24	9
Mr. Speaker resumes Chair in certain cases, without question put	164	25
When Chairman unable to continue in	171	26
Motion to leave the Chair : its effects	174	26
Use of Benches on either side of	12	9
CHAIRMAN OF COMMITTEES OF THE WHOLE HOUSE—		
Appointment of—vacancy in office of	8	7
Takes the Chair in unavoidable absence of Mr. Speaker	9	7
Takes the Chair in temporary absence of Mr. Speaker	10	7
Absence of, or when acting as Deputy Speaker	11	7
Reports that a quorum of Members is not present	27	10
Directs words to be taken down	114	19
When Chairman rises to speak, Member speaking to sit down	119	19
Maintains order	118	19
No motion of obstructive character that Chairman leave Chair	133	21
May order discontinuance of speech	134	21
May put motion " That the question be now put "	135	21
In case of equality of voices, to give casting vote	158	24
Directed to report conduct of Member	165, 166	25
Leaves Chair if want of quorum noticed	167	25
Reports when quorum is not present	169	26
May call upon any Member present to take his place	171	26
Orders withdrawal of strangers	333	46
Shall be directed to report	172	26
Reports Progress	173	26
Motion that Chairman leave Chair	174	26
CHAIRMAN OF SELECT COMMITTEE—		
Election of	192	28
Vote of	195	29
Prepares Report	204	30
Report to be signed by	206	30
On Private Bill has vote in first instance, and also casting vote	294	40
Charges against Member	214	31
Charge upon the people. *See* Supply.		
Citation of documents by Members	302	41
Clauses, new, at report stage	270, 271	37
Clerical error in Bills—J.S.O.	20	50
Clerk-Assistant carries message to the Legislative Council	223	32
„ of each House carries messages to the other—J.S.O.	2	47

	NO. OF RULE.	PAGE.
Clerk-Assistant of Legislative Council—J.S.O.	19	50
CLERK OF THE HOUSE—		
Or other person appointed, reads the Proclamation convening Parliament	1	5
Reads commission for swearing Members	3	5
Writs for general election of Members delivered to, on the opening of a new Parliament ...	2	6
Reads returns endorsed on writs for general election	2	6
Clerk addressed by Members when House proceeds to choice of Speaker	4	6
Puts question on choice of Speaker	6	6
Notices of motion delivered to	34	11
Reads Orders of the Day without any question put	55	13
The Clerk takes down words objected to, when directed by Mr. Speaker	113	19
The Clerk takes down words objected to, when directed by the Chairman	114	19
Reads Petitions when presented, if ordered ...	241	34
Reads amendments made in a Bill first time throughout, and a second time, on motion, one by one	269	37
Certifies to passing of Bills	278	38
Certifies to unusual majority in certain Bills ...	286	39
Certifies Order of the House for attendance of person charged with contempt	321	43
Votes and Proceedings of House and Committee noted and signed by	327	45
Takes record of attendance of Members	328	45
Furnishes printed Papers to Members	329	45
Has custody of Records	330	45
CLERK OF PARLIAMENTS—		
Authenticates Bills—J.S.O.	13	49
Presents all Bills except the Appropriation Bill—J.S.O.	14	49
Deposits Bills—J.S.O.	15	49
Clerk of Legislative Council shall be Clerk of the Parliaments	18	49
In case of absence or illness, duties to be performed by Clerk-Assistant of the Council—J.S.O. ...	19	50
Duties respecting correction of errors in Bills—J.S.O.	20	50
Command, Papers presented by	301	41
Commission for Opening Parliament : Course of Procedure	1, 2	5
Commission for swearing Members	3	5
COMMITTAL OF BILLS—		
To a Committee of the Whole House	254	35
Or to a Select Committee	254	35
COMMITTEES, JOINT—		
Of the Council and Assembly, Rules respecting—J.S.O.	8, 9	48
COMMITTEES, SELECT—		
No reference to proceedings of, until reported ...	129	20
Mr. Speaker not obliged to serve on...	183	27
Number of Members of which composed	184	27
Willingness of Members to attend to be ascertained	185	28

	NO. OF RULE.	PAGE.
COMMITTEES, SELECT—*continued.*		
Notice to specify names	186	28
Ballot may be ordered	187	28
Manner of balloting	188	28
List of Members serving	189	28
Members discharged and others appointed	190	28
Quorum	191	28
Election of Chairman	192	28
When quorum not present	193, 194	28, 29
Vote of Chairman	195	29
Power to send for persons, papers, and records	196	29
Days of meetings	197	29
Not to sit while House sitting	198	29
May adjourn from place to place	199	29
Names of Members present to be entered	200	29
Divisions to be entered	201	29
Admission and exclusion of strangers	202	29
Open to all Members of the House	203	29
Chairman to prepare report	204	30
Proceedings on consideration of draft report	205	30
Report to be signed by Chairman	206	30
Progress Reports	207	30
Evidence, &c., not to be published before reported	208	30
Instruction to	209	30
Witnesses not attending	210	30
Attendance of Members to be examined in	212	31
If Member refuse to attend	213	31
Charges against Member	214	31
Public Bill may be referred to Select Committee	254	35
On Private Bills	293 to 298	40
COMMITTEES OF THE WHOLE HOUSE—		
Appointment of Chairman	8	7
Chairman takes the Chair	154	24
Quorum of	26	9
When Chairman reports that quorum of Members is not present	27	10
Words taken down in Committee	114	19
Disorder arising in	118, 164	19, 25
No reference to proceedings of, until reported	129	20
No motion of obstructive character allowed in	133	21
Committee directs "That Question be now put"	135	21
Division lists entered in the Votes	143	23
Divisions taken and recorded in same manner as in Votes	150	23
Members personally interested may not vote	152	23
House resolves itself into Committee	153	24
Question put for Speaker to leave the Chair	154	24
Committee may be put off to any time	155	24
When the Committee has reported Progress, the Speaker leaves the Chair without any question	156	24
When Committee has reported Progress	156	24
Committee to consider only such matters as are referred to them	157	24
Questions decided by majority of votes	158	24

	NO. OF RULE.	PAGE.
COMMITTEES OF THE WHOLE HOUSE—continued.		
Motion in Committee is not seconded	48, 159	12, 24
Previous question not to be moved	160	24
Rules of Debate same as in House	161	24
Members may speak more than once	162	25
Greater or lesser sum, longer or shorter time	163	25
Members using objectionable words and not explaining or retracting	165	25
When quorum not present on Division	168	26
Disturbance by Members	166	25
Report made, when all matters referred have been considered	172	26
Report of Progress	173	26
Motion made during Committee to report Progress and ask leave to sit again	173	26
Motion that Chairman leave the Chair	174	26
Report to be brought up without question	175	26
Resolution cannot be postponed	176	26
Committee cannot adjourn	177	27
Resolutions of Committee	178	27
Effect of instruction	179	27
Instruction not to be moved as an amendment	180	27
When instruction moved after first sitting	181	27
Direction to report by a specified day	182	27
Any Member may put question to witness	219	31
Member takes notice that strangers are present	333	46
Vacancy in office of Chairman	8	7
COMMITTEES OF SUPPLY AND WAYS AND MEANS—		
No amendment entertained on going into, without leave	132	21
No motion of obstructive character allowed in	133	21
Opening of Committee of Supply	307	42
Estimates transmitted by message from Governor referred to	307	42
Committee of Ways and Means appointed	317	43
Resolutions reported from, received on future day	318	43
Manner in which resolutions dealt with	319	43
Committees. See also Chairman.		
Commons, House of, Rules and Practice of, adopted in any case not provided for by Standing Orders of the Assembly	325	44
J.S.O.	21	50
Complicated Question may be divided	72	15
Consequences of suspension of Member	331	46
Communication between the two Houses to be by message—J.S.O.	1	47
CONSTITUTION ACT—		
Witness summoned under sections forty-one and forty-two of	210	30
Bill for alteration of certain provisions of	286	39
Offences enumerated in the forty-fifth section of	321	43
Members sworn as prescribed by the	3	6
Form of warrant in words of	325	44

	NO. OF RULE.	PAGE.
CONTEMPT—		
Persons charged with, to be summoned	321	43
Proceedings if person charged attends	322	44
„ „ „ does not attend ...	323	44
Punishment of person adjudged guilty of	324	44
Member declared guilty of, committed to custody of Sergeant-at-Arms...	325	44
Fees payable on arrest... ... ... · ..; ...	326	44
Corporations, Petitions of	231	33
Council. See Legislative Council.		
Counsel heard by Select Committee on Private Bills ...	297	40
COUNTING OF THE HOUSE—		
If quorum of Members not present half-an-hour after time appointed for meeting, Mr. Speaker adjourns the House till the next sitting-day ...	24	9
When Chairman of Committees reports that a quorum is not present, Mr. Speaker counts the House and adjourns	27	10
Member held to be present during, who takes notice of want of quorum	29	10
Bell to be rung and doors unlocked while Mr. Speaker is counting	30	10
Mr. Speaker counts House when Chairman reports no quorum present	169	26
Cross benches on either side of the Chair	12	9
Custody of Records	330	45
„ persons ordered to be imprisoned	324, 325	44
D.		
Days of Meeting	23	9
DEBATES—		
Not allowed on formal business	61	13
„ putting questions to Members ...	64	14
„ answering questions	65	14
On previous question may be adjourned	78	15
Members to address Mr. Speaker	99	17
Member unable to stand may speak sitting	15	17
No Member to speak after voices given	100	17
Mr. Speaker calls upon Members to speak	101	17
Motion that a Member "be now heard," "be not heard," or "be not further heard"	102	17
When Member may speak	103	18
Explanation, personal	104	18
Member who has spoken may be heard to explain himself	105	18
No Member may speak twice to a question except in certain cases	106, 123	18, 20
Reply allowed in certain cases	107	18
Member not to interrupt another	108	18
Speaking "to order," or upon a matter of privilege	109	18
Question of Order, how dealt with	110	18
Member not to use offensive words in reference to another	111	18

	NO. OF RULE.	PAGE.
DEBATES—*continued.*		
Digression	112	18
Previous Debates of same Session may not be alluded to	112	18
Imputations of improper motives and all personal reflections are disorderly...	112	18
Objectionable words taken down in the House ...	113	19
„ words to be objected to when used ...	115	19
Members not explaining or retracting, censured ...	116	19
No noise or disturbance allowed during a debate ...	117	19
Means of maintaining order in the House and in Committee	118	19
When House to be silent	119	19
Adjournment of	121	19
Being resumed, Members not to speak again ...	122	20
Same Member not to move adjournment of House and of Debate	127	20
On motion for Adjournment of the House	130	20
Motion—" That Question be now put "	135	21
Right of reply when House directed that question " be now put "	136	22
Speaking " to order " during a Division	151	23
Rules in Committee, same as in the House	161	24
In Committee Members may speak more than once	162	25
Debate in Committee cannot be adjourned	177	27
Petition may not be presented during	224	32
On clause or amendment of Bill under discussion to be relevant	258	36
Deposit of twenty-five pounds in relation to Private Bill	292	40
Deputy-Speaker, House may appoint	12	7
„ Chairman	171	26
Discharge of Member from Select Committee	190	28
Discharged, Order of the House may be read and ...	82	15
Disorder in Committee to be reported to the House ...	118, 166	19, 25
„ House	117	19
„ on sudden, Mr. Speaker resumes the Chair ...	164	25
DIVISIONS—		
If Mr. Speaker's declaration not acquiesced in, question determined by	70	14
Sergeant-at-Arms rings a bell, and sand-glass turned	137	22
Doors closed	138	22
No Member may vote unless present when the question is put	139	22
Every Member then present must vote	140	22
Tellers appointed	141	22
If not two Tellers, no Division	142	22
Lists entered in the Votes	143	23
Tellers report the numbers	144	23
In case of confusion or error, House again divides...	145	23
Mistakes in	146, 149	23
When votes equal, Mr. Speaker gives casting vote ...	147	23
Demanded only by minority	148	23
Members having given voices, not to vote differently on Division	149	23

	NO. OF RULE.	PAGE.
DIVISIONS—*continued.*		
In Committee	150	23
,, when Quorum not present	168	26
Question of Order during	151	23
Members not entitled to vote if personally interested	152	23
In Select Committees, to be entered	201	29
Documents read or cited by Members	302	41
Doors kept unlocked when House is being counted ...	30	10
Doors closed in Divisions •	138	22
E.		
Election, General, writs for	*2	6
,, of Speaker	4, 5, 6	6
,, Chairman of Select Committees	192	28
Enacting Authority, Form of Statement of, in Public Bills	17	34
Equality of Votes. *See* Casting Votes.		
Error, clerical, discovered in any Bill after passing—J.S.O.	20	50
Estimate or item in Supply may be postponed ...	316	43
Estimates referred to the Committee of Supply ...	307	42
Evidence, &c., in Select Committee not to be published before reported	208	31
Explanation of words, Member who has already spoken may be again heard in	104, 105	18
F.		
Fees imposed by Legislative Council in Bills	306	41
,, payable on arrest of person guilty of con empt ...	326	44
First Reading of a Bill	246, 247	34
Formal or unopposed business	59	13
,, ,, ,, amendment or debate not allowed on	61	13
,, Motions and Orders take precedence	60	13
,, ,, ,, do not prevent other business	62	14
G.		
Galleries, admission of strangers to	332	46
Gazette, notice to apply for Private Bill to be published in	287	39
General Election, writs for	2	6
Government days, order of business on	58	13
GOVERNOR—		
Proclamation by, convening Parliament	1	5
House attends in Council Chamber	10	7
Addresses to, how presented	17	8
,, answer to, to be reported	18	8
Messages from	{ 164, 220 221 }	25, 32
Amendments proposed by, in Bills	284	38
When Governor's amendments are agreed to, to be sent to Legislative Council	285	39

	NO. OF RULE.	PAGE.
GOVERNOR'S SPEECH—		
On receipt of a message to attend Governor in Council, Mr. Speaker with the House proceeds to the Legislative Council	10	7
On returning, Mr. Speaker reports that Governor made speech	11	8
A Bill read pro formâ before Speech is reported ...	13	8
Mr. Speaker reports Governor's Speech	13	8
Address in Reply ... ... ·... ...	14, 15	8
Speech ordered to be taken into consideration ...	16	8
Referred to Committee of Supply	307	42
Greater or lesser sum, longer or shorter time	163	25
Grievances, petitions complaining of	243	34

H.

HOUSE—		
Same Member not to move adjournment of debate and	127	20
Member proposed as Speaker submits himself to the	4	6
To adjourn after Election of Speaker	6	6
Rights and privileges of, confirmed	8, 9	6, 7
Attends Governor in Council Chamber	10	7
May proceed without quorum when no notice taken	13	11
Members entering or leaving...	20, 22	9
Use of benches on either side of	12	9
Adjourned if quorum not present	24, 25	9
Will not proceed to business until half-an-hour after time appointed to sit	24	9
Adjourned on its own resolution	31	10
Whole, Committee of. See Committees.		
Counted	24, 27	9, 10
Words taken down in	113	19
Of Commons Rules adopted	335	46

I.

Imputation of improper motives	112	18
INSTRUCTIONS—		
Effect of, to a Committee of the Whole House ...	179	27
Not to be moved as an amendment	180	27
When moved after first sitting	181	27
Direction to report by a specified day	182	27
Effect of, to Select Committee	209	30
Interest, personal, of Member voting	152	23
INTERRUPTION OF DEBATES—		
Member making personal explanation may, by leave, interrupt another Member	108	18
Business of House suspended by message from the Governor	220	32
Introduction of Members not elected at a General Election	19	8
Irrelevance of speech	134	21
Items, motions respecting, in Committee of Supply ...	{ 311 to 316 }	42, 43

—	NO. OF RULE.	PAGE.

J.

Joint Committees, Rules respecting—J.S.O. ...	8, 9	48
JOINT STANDING ORDERS—		
I.—*Messages.*		
Communications to be by Message	1	47
To be transmitted by Clerk-Assistant, unless otherwise ordered	2	47
Members carrying message	3	47
Message carried by Clerk	4	47
Consent desired to Bills, Votes, and Resolutions, how communicated	5	48
Same course when returning	6	48
Amendments insisted on and communications desired, reasons	7	48
Joint Committees	8, 9	48
II.—*Bills.*		
Bills to be fair printed, as certified	10	49
Amendments to be written on paper, and certified by the Clerk	11	49
Government Printer to furnish three copies of Bills, on vellum, to Clerk of Parliaments	12	49
Fair prints to be authenticated by Clerk of Parliaments	13	49
Clerk of Parliaments to present all Bills, except Appropriation Bill, to the Governor	14	49
Disposal of original Bills	15	49
Title of Bill	16	49
Bills to be numbered	17	50
Clerk of the Parliaments	18	50
Clerk-Assistant of Legislative Council to perform duties, in case of absence of Clerk of Parliaments	19	50
Clerical error in Bills	20	50
Practice of Imperial Parliament	21	50
JOURNALS OF THE HOUSE	327	45
Record of attendance of Members entered in ...	328	45

L.

Lapsed Motions	46, 48	12
„ Orders may be restored	57	13
Laws, Temporary	280	38
Leave, Motions without notice by...	47	12
LEGISLATIVE COUNCIL—		
On receiving message from Commissioners, Members proceed to Council Chamber	2	6
House attends Governor in, Chamber	10	7
Attendance of Member or Officer, as witness ...	215	31
Message from, how received	222	32
„ to, how communicated	223	32
Bills brought from	248	35
„ sent to	281	38
Amendments to Bills	282, 283	38

—	NO. OF RULE.	PAGE.
LEGISLATIVE COUNCIL—_continued._		
Governor's amendments sent to	285	39
Private Bill coming from the ...	295	40
See also Messages, Bills, Private Bills, Joint Standing Orders, and Supply		
LIBRARY—		
Joint Committee to be appointed—J.S.O.	8	48

M.

Main Question, Member who has spoken on Question of Adjournment may speak to	124	20
„ „ not to be entered upon, on Question of Adjournment	125	20
Majority of voices determine Question	69	14
„ Speaker declares	70	14
„ unusual, required in passing Bills	286	39
Meeting, days of	23	9
„ of Select Committees	197	29
Member proposed as Speaker	4	6
Proposed as Speaker, submits himself to the House	4	6
MEMBERS—		
On opening of a new Parliament, assemble in the House	1	5
Members await message from Commissioners	1	5
On receipt of message, proceed to Council Chamber	2	5
Commissioners for swearing	3	5
Sworn	3	6
Introduction of, not elected at General Election	19	8
Make obeisance to Chair	20	9
Leaving their seats may not pass between Chair and Member speaking, nor between Chair and Table	21	9
Entering the House	22	9
Rules regulating the places of	22	9
Taking notice of want of quorum shall be counted	29	10
May put questions to any other Member	63	14
Unable to stand may speak sitting	15	17
When two or more, rise to speak	101	17
Motion that Member "be now heard," "be not heard," &c.	102	17
May not use offensive words against another Member	111	18
Objecting to words used in debate	113, 114	19
Not explaining or retracting	116	19
Shall not make any noise or disturbance	117	19
Speaking to sit down when Mr. Speaker or Chairman rises	119	19
To withdraw while conduct under consideration	120	19
Question to, may be referred to on Motion for Adjournment	130	20
Not explaining or retracting objectionable words in Committee	165	25
Disturbance by, in Committee	166	25
Select Committee open to all	203	29
Attendance of, to be examined as witness in House or Committee of the Whole	211	31

—	NO. OF RULE.	PAGE.
MEMBERS—*continued.*		
Attendance of, to be examined as witness before Select Committee	212	31
If Member refuse to attend	213	31
Charges against	214	31
Member shall be examined in his place	218	31
Any Member may put questions in Committee	219	31
Presenting Petition to affix his name	235	33
„ „ previously to peruse same	234	33
To take care that Petition is in conformity with the Rules	236	33
Certifies to translation of Petition not in English language	228	32
Petitions must be presented by	238	33
Cannot present Petition from himself	239	33
Confined to statement of certain facts in presenting Petition	240	33
Document read or cited by, may be ordered to be tabled	302	41
Declared guilty of contempt shall be committed	325	44
Record of attendance of, entered in Votes and Proceedings	328	45
Copies of Papers for	329	45
Consequences of suspension of	331	46
Takes notice that strangers are present	333	46
See also Roll.		
MESSAGES FROM THE GOVERNOR—		
If House in Committee when announced, Speaker resumes Chair	164	25
When announced, business suspended	220	32
Read by Mr. Speaker	221	32
Message from Commissioners—		
Appointed for opening Parliament	1	5
On receiving, Members proceed to Council Chamber	2	5
MESSAGES BETWEEN THE TWO HOUSES—		
Message for attendance of Member or Officer of Council as witness	215	31
From the Council, how received	222	32
To the Council, how communicated	223	32
All communications between the Council and Assembly shall be by—J.S.O.	1	47
Unless otherwise directed, shall be communicated by Clerk-Assistant—J.S.O.	2	47
Members carrying messages—J.S.O.	3	47
Messages carried by Clerk—J.S.O.	4	47
Respecting Bills, Votes, and Resolutions—J.S.O.	5, 6, 7	48
Minority only can demand Division	148	23
Mistakes in Divisions corrected in Votes	146	23
Money Bills, how initiated	245	34
„ Petition for granting	308	42
„ Address to the Crown for	310	42

F

	NO. OF RULE.	PAGE.
MOTIONS—		
Notices of, not disposed of at the time of Adjournment	.32	10
Notices of, and Orders of the Day, private, take precedence alternately	33	10
Notices of, fair copy of, to be delivered at Table ...	34	11
Notices of, not to be given for same day, or more than eight days in advance	35	11
Notices of, may be given by proxy	36	11
Notices to be printed with Votes	37	11
Notices of, terms may be altered	38	11
Fresh notice may be given for later but not for an earlier day...	39	11
Time for giving Notices of	40	11
Notices set down in order in which they are given ...	41	12
Urgent, concerning Privilege, take precedence	42	12
Notices of, may be expunged...	43	12
Motion for Vote of Thanks has precedence ...	14	12
Notices of, necessary to initiate subject for discussion	44	12
For printing of Papers presented by Command, &c.	45	12
Order of	46	12
Not made, lapse	46	12
By leave without notice	47	12
Not seconded shall lapse in certain cases	48	12
May be withdrawn by leave	49	12
Withdrawn by leave, may be made again	50	12
Original, shall not be withdrawn until Amendment disposed of	52	13
Notices of, relating to business of the House take precedence...	62	13
That Member "be now heard," "be not heard," &c.	102	17
Member who has spoken may not make, but may speak to, new Motion	126	20
Restrictions upon, for Adjournment of the House...	130,131	20, 21
Of an obstructive character in Committee	133	21
"That Question be now put"...	135	21
Need not be seconded in Committee ...	159	24
To leave the Chair in Committee, supersedes proceedings	174	26
Not to be withdrawn in absence of proposer	51	12
Formal, take precedence of all others	60	13
„ no Amendment or Debate allowed on	61	14
„ do not prevent other business	62	14
Irregular, not proposed	67	14
For any public aid or charge upon the people	309	42
For address to the Crown praying that money may be issued ...	310	42
In Committee of Supply, to omit or reduce item ...	311 to 316	42, 43
Motives, imputation of	112	18

N.

| Names to be specified in Motion for Select Committee ... | 186 | 28 |
| New Member, introduction of | 19 | 8 |

	NO. OF RULE.	PAGE.
Notice, when no, taken, House may proceed without quorum	13	11
NOTICES OF MOTION—		
Not disposed of at time of Adjournment	32	10
Private, and Orders of the Day take precedence alternately...	33	10
Relating to business of the House shall take precedence of all other business	33	10
Fair copy to be delivered at Table	34	11
Not to be given for same day, or more than eight days in advance	35	11
A Member may give notice for another Member ...	36	11
Every Notice printed and circulated with Votes ...	37	11
Terms may be altered...	38	11
Fresh notice may be given for later but not for earlier day	39	11
Not to be given after business begun	40	11
Set down in order in which they are given	41	12
Notices containing unbecoming expressions expunged	43	12
Necessary to initiate subject of discussion	44	12
Printing of Papers without	45	12
Motions may be made without, by leave	47	12
And Orders arranged by Government on Government days...	58	13
Relating to business of House, take precedence ...	62	13
For appointment of a Select Committee	186	28
To be given of new clauses on consideration of Bill as amended	270	37
Of amendments on recommittal	274	37
See also Motions.		

O.

OATH—		
of Allegiance, Members take...	3	6
Witnesses examined on, only in cases provided for by Statute...	16	31
Obeisance made by Members to the Chair in passing to or from their seats	20	9
Objection to words to be made immediately	115	19
OBJECTIONABLE WORDS—		
Member not explaining or retracting	116	19
„ „ „ in Committee	165	25
Offences under the "*Constitution Act of* 1867" ...	321	43
OFFENSIVE WORDS—		
A Member shall not use, in reference to another Member	111	18
Opening of Parliament, proceedings on	1 to 6	5, 6
ORDER—		
Of Motions	46	12
Any Member may rise to speak to	103, 109	18
A question of, how dealt with	110	18
Mr. Speaker preserves, in the House	117, 118	19
The Chairman preserves in the Committee	118	19
Question of, during Division	151	20

xviii. INDEX.

—	NO. OF RULE.	PAGE.
ORDER OF THE HOUSE—		
May be rescinded	81	15
May be read and discharged	82	15
ORDERS OF THE DAY—		
Not disposed of at time of Adjournment	32	10
And Notices, private, take precedence alternately	33	10
Need not be seconded	48	12
	56	13
Definition of	53	13
Disposed of in the order in which they stand upon paper	54	13
Mr. Speaker directs The Clerk to read, without question put	55	13
Lapsed, may be restored	57	13
Order of business on Government days	58	13
Formal, take precedence	60	13
No Amendment or Debate on	61	14
Disposal of, does not prevent other business	62	14
Amendment to, must be relevant	97	17
Orders. *See* Standing Rules and Orders.		

P.

PAPERS—		
Printing of, without notice	45	12
May be ordered to be laid upon the Table	299	41
Address for	300	41
Presented by Statute or by Command	301	41
Ordered to be Printed	305	41
Copies of, for Members	329	45
Parliament Buildings—Joint Committee to be appointed to manage—J.S O.	8	48
Parliament, proceedings on opening	1 to 6	5, 6
PARLIAMENT, IMPERIAL—		
Practice of	335	46
J S.O.	21	50
PARLIAMENTS, CLERK OF—		
Duties of, defined—J.S.O.	12 to 15, 17, 20	49 50
The Clerk of the Legislative Council shall be	18	50
In case of absence or illness of, duties to be performed by Clerk-Assistant of the Council— J.S.O.	19	50
Duties of, in discovery of errors in Bills defined— J.S.O.	20	50
Passing of Bills	276	38
„ Clerk to certify to	278	38
Payment in relation to Private Bills	292	40
Pecuniary interest of Member voting	152	23
Penalties, forfeiture, and fees, Bill brought from the Legislative Council relating to	306	41
Personal explanations, Members allowed to make	104, 105	18
Personal reflections shall be deemed highly disorderly	112	18
Personal interest of Member voting	152	23

	NO. OF RULE.	PAGE.
PETITIONS, PUBLIC—		
When to be presented...	224	32
To be written or printed	225	32
To contain a prayer at the end	226	32
To be signed on the same sheet or skin	227	32
To be in English, or with a certified translation ...	228	32
To be signed by the parties	229	33
Signatures not to be transferred	230	33
Of corporations	231	33
No letters, affidavits, &c., to be attached	232	33
No application for public money, unless recommended by the Crown	233	33
Nor for compounding debts due to the Crown ...	233	33
Nor for remission of duties	233	33
Member presenting, previously to peruse same ...	234	33
Member to affix his name	235	33
Member to take care it is in conformity with the rules	236	33
To be respectful	237	33
To be presented by Members only	238	33
Member cannot present, from himself	239	33
Members confined to statement of certain facts ...	240	33
Not to be debated, but may be read by The Clerk...	241	34
May be ordered to be received	242	34
Complaining of grievances	243	34
For granting money, considered in Committee ...	308	42
Petitions for Private Bills	{ 288, 289, 290	39
„ against Private Bills	296	40
PLACES OF MEMBERS—		
Rules and Orders regulating the same	21, 22	9
Use of Benches on either side of the House ...	12	9
Practice of Imperial Parliament—J.S.O.	21	50
„ adopted in any case not provided for by Standing Orders	335	46
Preamble of Bill to be postponed to the last	255	35
„ „ considered, and, if necessary, amended	265	36
Precedence given to Vote of Thanks	14	12
„ alternately, of Private Notices and Orders...	33	10
„ given to Questions of Privilege	42	12
„ given to Formal Motions and Orders ...	60	13
Prerogative. *See* Royal Prerogative.		
PREVIOUS QUESTION—		
Question superseded by the	73	15
Precludes amendment unless withdrawn	74	15
If resolved in the negative, main question put ...	75	15
The question for the, may be superseded by the Adjournment of the House	76	15
Cannot be amended	76	15
Not to be moved upon amendment	77	15
Debate upon, may be adjourned	78	15
When not to be moved	79	15
Proposed on series of resolutions decided by first ...	80	15
Not to be moved in Committee	160	24

	NO. OF RULE.	PAGE.
PRINTING—		
Of Papers without notice	45	12
Committee, appointment of	304	41
Of Accounts and Papers	305	41
Private Notices of Motion and Orders of the Day take		
precedence alternately	33	10
PRIVATE BILLS—		
Notice to apply for, to be published in *Gazette* ...	287	39
Initiation of	288	39
Petition for, to set forth that due Notice has been		
published, &c.	289	39
When Petition has been received	290	39
Printed at expense of persons applying	291	39
When leave to bring in, has been obtained	291	39
Deposit of twenty-five pounds	292	40
To be referred to Select Committee	293	40
Chairman's vote	294	40
Coming from Legislative Council	295	40
Petitions against	296	40
A Select Committee may hear counsel	297	40
Mode of procedure in Select Committee	297	40
When Select Committee has reported in favour ...	298	40
Penalties, forfeitures, and fees imposed by Legisla-		
tive Council	306	41
PRIVILEGES—		
Questions of, take precedence	42	12
Member may speak to matter of	109	18
Petition containing matter in breach of	241	34
Rights and privileges of the House, Speaker lays		
claim to	8	6
Speaker reports the confirmation of	9	7
Proclamation on opening Parliament	1	5
Progress Reports from Committee of the Whole ...	173, 182	26, 27
„ „ of Select Committees	207	30
Proxy, notice of motion may be given by	36	11
Public aid, motion for	309	42
„ Bills. *See* Bills.		
Punishment of person adjudged guilty of contempt ...	324	44

Q.

Quarrels not to be prosecuted	18	44
QUESTION—		
No debate allowed on putting to Members	64	14
Member shall not debate matter in answering ...	65	14
Question proposed by Mr. Speaker when a motion		
has been made and seconded	66	14
Not proposed when motion or amendment is irregu-		
lar or out of order	67	14
Put by Mr. Speaker when debate is ended	68	14
If not heard, Mr. Speaker will state it again ...	68	14
Determined by a majority of voices	69	14
Mr. Speaker states whether "Ayes" or "Noes"		
have it; but if this is not acquiesced in, a Divi-		
sion ensues	70	14

	NO. OF RULE.	PAGE.
QUESTION—*continued.*		
The same, not proposed again in the same Session	71	14
Complicated, may be divided	71	15
Superseded by adjournment	73	15
„ by amendments	73	15
„ by passing to some other business	73	15
„ by the Previous Question	73	15
No Member to speak to, after the same has been *put* and voices taken	100	17
No Member to speak twice to the same	106, 122	18, 20
Main, Member may speak to, after having spoken to adjournment	124	20
Main, not to be entered upon on question of adjournment	125	20
That Member be further heard	134	21
Motion, "That the Question be now put"	135	21, 22
Right of reply when House directed that the question " be now put "	136	22
See also "Previous Question."		
QUESTIONS PUT TO MEMBERS—		
To Ministers of the Crown and others	63	14
Reference may be made to, on motion for adjournment	130	20, 21
Any Member may put, to witness in Committee	219	31
Questions of privilege take precedence	42	12
QUESTIONS OF ORDER—		
Arising out of debate	103	18
Member may rise to speak to	109	18
How dealt with	110	18
During Division	151	23
QUORUM—		
If not present within half-an-hour, Mr. Speaker adjourns House	24	9
When not present after business, Mr. Speaker adjourns House	25	9
Of Committee of the Whole House	26	9
When Chairman reports not present, Mr. Speaker shall count the House	27	10
And if not present, he shall adjourn the House	27	10
Member taking notice of want of, shall be counted	29	10
Disposal of business when House adjourns for want of	32	10
House proceeds without, when no notice taken	13	11
If want of, in Committee, Chairman leaves Chair	167	25
When not present on Division in Committee	168	26
Chairman reports when not present	169	26
Duty of Mr. Speaker when a, not present in Committee	169	26
If present when House counted	170	26
Of Select Committee	191	28
When not present	193, 194	28, 29

	NO. OF RULE.	PAGE.

R.

	NO. OF RULE.	PAGE.
Recommittal, consideration of amendments to Bill on	272	37
„ on third reading	273	37
Records, custody of, in the Clerk	330	45
Reduction proposed in Committee of Supply	315	43
Reflections, personal, shall be deemed highly disorderly	112	18
Refreshment rooms, Joint Committee to be appointed to manage—J.S.O.	8	48
Repeal of Standing Rules and Orders heretofore made...	336	46
Relevancy of debate on clauses or amendments to Bills	258	36
REPLY (IN DEBATE)—		
Allowed in certain cases	107	18
Right of	136	22
REPORTS FROM COMMITTEES OF THE WHOLE—		
No reference to proceedings of Committees until reported	129	20
When all matters referred have been considered, Chairman shall be directed to report	172	26
Report of Progress	173	26
Report to be brought up without question	175	26
Resolutions of Committee	178	27
Direction to report by a specified day	182	27
Title of Bill amended to be specially reported ...	260	36
Report of Bill	266	36
„ „ without amendment	267	37
„ „ with amendments	268	37
New clauses or schedules at report stage	271	37
REPORT FROM SELECT COMMITTEES—		
Chairman to prepare	204	30
Proceedings on consideration of	205	30
Manner in which brought up	206	30
Progress and special	207	30
On Private Bill	298	40
Rescission of votes	81	15
RESOLUTIONS FROM COMMITTEES OF SUPPLY AND WAYS AND MEANS—		
To be received on future day	318	43
Manner in which dealt with	319	43
Amendment to (in Supply), increasing charge on people, not to be made	320	43
RESOLUTIONS—		
When previous question proposed on series of ...	80	15
May be rescinded	81	15
Cannot be postponed	176	26
Of Committees of the Whole	178	27
Restriction of motions for adjournment ... }	130 131	20 21
Resumption of debate, Member not to speak again on ...	122	20
Returns, unfurnished	303	41
Right of reply	107, 136	18, 22
Rights and Privileges—		
Of the House, Speaker lays claim to	8	6
Speaker reports confirmation of	9	7
Roll of Members, Members sign	3, 19	6, 8

	NO. OF RULE.	PAGE.
Rotation of Orders of the Day	**54**	13
„ of Motions	**41**	12
Rules. *See* "Standing Rules and Orders."		
Royal approbation of Speaker elect	**7, 8, 9**	6, 7
Royal Prerogative, when concerned in any account or paper	**300**	41

S.

Sand-glass to be turned, in Divisions	**137**	22
Schedules to Bill	**262-264**	36
„ „ new, at report stage of	**270, 271**	37
Seconded, motion need not be, in Committee	**159**	24
SECOND READING OF BILLS—		
Ordered on a future day	**249**	35
Question for, put	**250**	35
Amendments to question for	**251**	35
Select Committees. *See* Committees, Select.		
SERGEANT-AT-ARMS—		
In Divisions to ring the bell	**137**	22
Messenger from Council introduced by	**222**	32
Person adjudged guilty of contempt committed to custody of	**324, 325**	44
Sickness or infirmity, Member unable to stand from, may speak sitting	**15**	17
SPEAKER—		
On opening of a new Parliament, course pursued in election of	**4, 5, 6**	6
Elect, conducted to Chair, returns acknowledgments, and is congratulated	**5**	6
On being called to Chair, expresses sense of honour proposed to be conferred on him, and submits himself	**6**	6
Presents himself for Royal approbation	**7**	6
Lays claim to rights and privileges of the House ...	**8**	6
Reports the Royal approbation and Confirmation of rights and privileges	**9**	7
Vacancy in office of	**7**	7
Unavoidable absence of, at meeting of the House ...	**9**	7
Temporary absence of, during sitting	**10**	7
Deputy, House may appoint	**12**	7
With the House goes up to Legislative Council to hear the Governor's Speech	**10**	7
On return from Council Chamber, makes report ...	**11**	8
Reports Governor's Speech	**13**	8
Part thereof again read by, on House proceeding to consider the same	**16**	8
Presents Address to Governor	**17**	8
Reports Answers	**17**	8
Counts House within half-an-hour after meeting, and if quorum not present adjourns House ...	**24**	9
While counting the House, bell rung and doors unlocked	**30**	10

	NO. OF RULE.	PAGE.
SPEAKER—*continued.*		
Directs the Clerk to read the Orders of the Day, without question put	55	13
Proposes the question to the House	66	14
If irregular, not proposed	67	14
If not heard, will again state it	68	14
When question put, states whether, in his opinion, the "Ayes" or the "Noes" have it	69, 141	14, 22
If his opinion not acquiesced in, a Division ensues...	70	14
Members whilst speaking to address themselves to	99	17
Calls upon a Member to speak when more than one rises	101	17
Shall give his opinion on question of Order... ...	110	18
Will direct words objected to, to be taken down ...	113	19
Censures Member not explaining or retracting objectionable words	116	19
Maintains order in the House	117, 118	19
When, rises during a debate, Member speaking sits down	119	19
Shall not put motion for Adjournment of the House unless five Members support it	130	20
May order discontinuance of speech...	134	21
Puts question forthwith without debate in certain cases	135	21, 22
Directs doors to be closed in Divisions	138	22
On Division directs the "Ayes" to the right and the "Noes" to the left, and appoints tellers ...	141	22
If not two tellers on one side, forthwith declares the resolution of the House	142	22
Declares numbers reported in Divisions	144	22
When equality of votes, gives casting vote	147	22
Puts question for leaving the Chair on House first going into Committee	154	24
Leaves the Chair without question put on order for further consideration of Bill or other matter in Committee...	156	24
Resumes the Chair in certain cases without question put	164	25
If want of quorum noticed in Committee, resumes the Chair	167	25
When quorum not present on Division in Committee, Mr. Speaker resumes the Chair...	168	26
Counts the House and adjourns when Chairman of Committees reports that a quorum not present	169	26
Not obliged to serve on Select Committees	183	27
Decides in an equality of votes for Members to serve on Select Committees	188	28
Witnesses before House examined by	216	31
Message from Governor to be read by	221	32
Has sole privilege of admitting strangers	332	33
Orders the withdrawal of strangers	333	33
Signs Votes and Proceedings...	327	45
SPEECH—		
Governor's, on opening session	11	8
Governor's	13, 14, 15, 16	8

	NO. OF RULE.	PAGE.
SPEECH—*continued.*		
Mr. Speaker or Chairman may order Member to discontinue	134	21
STANDING RULES AND ORDERS—		
May be suspended	334	46
In all cases not specially provided for by, House of Commons Rules adopted...	335	46
Repeal of	336	46
See also J.S.O.		
Statute, Papers presented by	301	41
STRANGERS—		
Admission of, to Select Committees	202	29
Admisssion of, to House by Mr. Speaker's Order ...	332	46
Ordered to withdraw from House	333	46
Withdrawal of, from House	333	46
Sum, greater or lesser	163	25
Superseded, questions how	73	15
SUPPLY, AND WAYS AND MEANS—		
On Governor's Speech being considered, motion made that the House will resolve itself into Committee of	16	8
No amendment on going into Committee without leave	132	21
No motion of obstructive character allowed in ...	133	21
Reports brought up only on question put	175	26
Penalties, forfeitures, and fees	306	41
Cases in which the House will not insist on its privileges	306	41
Opening of Committee of	307	42
Petitions, motion, or Bill for granting money, &c., proceeded upon in Committee only	308	42
Motion relating to money not to be presently entered upon, but a future day appointed	309	42
Motion for address to the Crown praying for money may be issued	310	42
Motion in Committee to omit or reduce item ...	311	42
Order in which motions are taken	312	42
After question for omitting item, no motion allowed on preceding item...	313	42
Proposition to omit or reduce item	314	42
When reduction is proposed	315	43
Postponement of estimate or item	316	43
Committee of Ways and Means constituted ...	317	43
Resolutions to be received on future day	318	43
Manner in which resolutions are dealt with ...	319	43
Charge on people, not to be increased	320	43
SUSPENSION OF—		
Member for conduct in the House	116, 117	19
„ in Committee	165, 166	25
„ consequences of	331	46
Standing Orders	334	46
Swearing Members, Commission for	3	5

	NO. OF RULE.	PAGE.
T.		
TABLE—		
Member may not pass between Chair and	21	9
Fair copy of Notice of Motion to be delivered at ...	34	11
Taxes, Bills imposing, shall be initiated in Committee ...	245	34
TELLERS—		
Two tellers on a Division appointed from each side	141	22
If not two tellers on one side, no Division	142	22
Tellers report numbers	144	23
Temporary laws	280	38
Terms of Notice of Motion may be altered	38	11
Thanks, Vote of, precedence given to motion for ...	14	12
Time, longer or shorter	163	25
THIRD READING OF BILL	273	37
Amendments or recommittal on	274	37
May be discharged	274	37
Question for	275	37
Further proceedings on, may be adjourned	277	38
TITLES OF BILL—		
Amended	259	36
Agreed to, after Bill read a third time and passed...	276	38
J.S.O.	16	49
Trade, Bills relating to finance or, initiated in Committee	245	34
U.		
Unfurnished Returns	303	41
Urgent motions take precedence	42	11
V.		
VACANCY—		
In office of Speaker	7	7
„ „ Chairman	8	7
VOTES, CASTING—		
Of Speaker	147	23
Of Chairman	158	24
Of Chairman of a Select Committee on Private Bill	294	40
VOICES—		
Questions determined by a majority of voices ...	69	14
Mr. Speaker states which has it; if his opinion not acquiesced in, a Division ensues...	70	14
No speaking after voices taken	100	17
Only Member who given against majority declared by Mr. Speaker can demand Division	148	23
Members having given, not to vote differently on Division	149	23
VOTE—		
Of the House may be rescinded	81	15
Of Members in Division	139, 140	22
Equality of	147	23
Of Chairman of Select Committee	195	29

	NO. OF RULE.	PAGE.
VOTES AND PROCEEDINGS—		
Notices of Motion to be printed with	37	11
Division lists in House and Committee entered in	143	23
Mistakes in Divisions corrected in	146	23
Every vote and proceeding entered by the Clerk at the Table	327	45
Ordered to be printed...	327	45
Shall be the Journals of the House	327	45
Record of attendance of Members entered in ...	328	45
Votes of Thanks, precedence given to motions for ...	12	12

W.

	NO. OF RULE.	PAGE.
WAYS AND MEANS—		
No amendment on going into Committee of, without leave	132	21
No motion of obstructive character allowed in ...	133	21
Reports brought up only on question put	175	26
Committee of, appointed	317	43
Resolution of, to be received on future day ...	318	43
Manner in which Resolutions dealt with	319	43
Withdrawal of motions is permitted by leave of the House	58	13
Withdrawal of strangers	333	46
Withdrawn motion may be made again	50	12
Withdrawn, motion or amendment may ... be, in absence of proposer ... ... -	51	12
WITNESSES—		
Duly summoned ; not attending	210	30
Attendance of Members to be examined	211, 212	30
If a Member refuse to attend...	213	31
Message for attendance of Member or Officer of Legislative Council	215	31
Not examined on oath except in certain cases ...	16	31
Examined by Mr. Speaker	216	31
To withdraw during discussion	217	31
A Member shall be examined in his place	218	31
Any Member may put questions in Committee ...	219	31
WORDS—		
Member shall not use unbecoming or offensive, in reference to another	111	18
Taken down in the House	113	19
Taken down in Committee reported to the House ...	114	19
Objection to, to be made immediately	115	19
Objectionable, Member not explaining or retracting	116	19
" " " in Committee	165	24
Writs for General Election	2	6

By Authority : JAMES C. BEAL, Government Printer, Brisbane.

EVERY MEMBER THEN PRESENT MUST VOTE.

(Approved by His Excellency The Governor, 12th September, 1893, in substitution for original Standing Order 140.)

140. Every Member present in the House when the Question is put with the doors closed shall vote.

RESOLUTIONS OF COMMITTEE.

(Approved by His Excellency The Governor, 12th September, 1893, in substitution for original Standing Order 178.)

178. Resolutions reported from a Committee of the whole House shall be read by the Clerk throughout without a Question, and may be agreed to or disagreed to by the House, or agreed to with Amendments, or recommitted to the Committee; or the further consideration thereof may be postponed.

CLAUSES MADE PART OF BILL.

(Approved by His Excellency The Governor, 12th September, 1893, in substitution for original Standing Orders 263 and 264.)

263. A Clause or Schedule, proposed to be added in Committee, shall be read by the Chairman, who shall then put the Question, "That the Clause (or Schedule) do stand part of the Bill"; and the Clause or Schedule may thereupon be amended or otherwise dealt with as in other cases.

Standing Order No. 269—"AMENDMENTS, HOW DEALT WITH"—repealed.

NEW CLAUSES AT REPORT STAGE.

(Approved by His Excellency The Governor, 12th September, 1893, in substitution for original Standing Order 271.)

271. If a Clause or Schedule is proposed to be added on consideration of the Bill as amended the Question shall be put, "That the Clause (or Schedule) do stand part of the Bill," and the Clause or Schedule may thereupon be amended or otherwise dealt with as in other cases.

www.ingramcontent.com/pod-product-compliance
Lightning Source LLC
Chambersburg PA
CBHW021524270326
41930CB00008B/1077